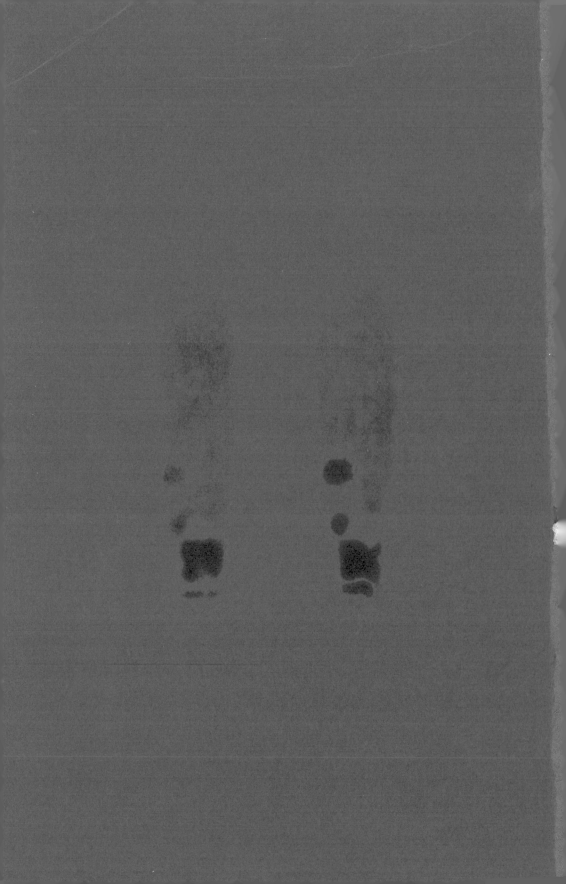

RECOLLECTIONS
OF A
BASEBALL
JUNKIE

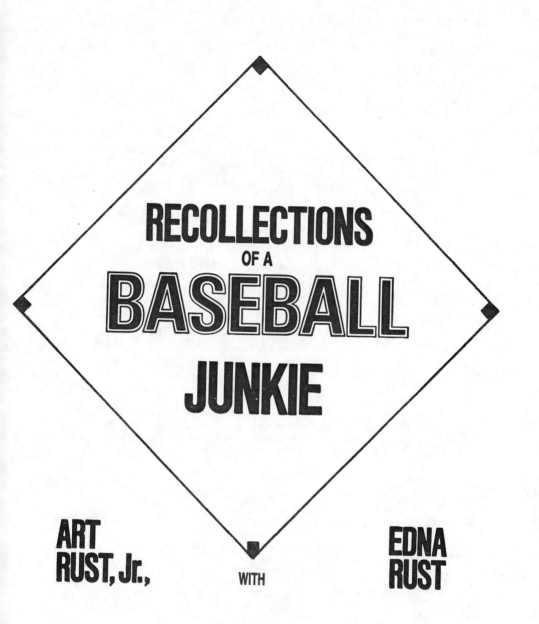

RECOLLECTIONS
OF A
BASEBALL
JUNKIE

ART RUST, Jr., WITH **EDNA RUST**

WILLIAM MORROW AND COMPANY, INC.
NEW YORK

To my mother, Edna Morgan, who always encouraged me
and said that I was right even when I was wrong.
—Edna Rust

To my mother-in-law for having the good taste to
produce my wife.
—Art Rust, Jr.

Library of Congress Cataloging in Publication Data

Rust, Art, 1927–
Recollections of a baseball junkie.

Includes index.
1. Baseball—United States—History.   2. Afro-
Americans—Social conditions.   3. Rust, Art, 1927–
4. Broadcasters—United States—Biography.
I. Rust, Edna.   II. Title.
GV863.A1R87   1985   070.4'49796'0924 [B]   84-25568
ISBN 0-688-03107-2

Printed in the United States of America

First Edition

1 2 3 4 5 6 7 8 9 10

BOOK DESIGN BY JAYE ZIMET

CONTENTS

THE SHADOW OF THE POLO GROUNDS AND OTHER ASSORTED PLACES

My first awareness of major league baseball was in 1933. My father was listening on our Stromberg-Carlson radio to the New York Giants and Washington Senators World Series. Of course I divined that much later. I really didn't understand World Series, or a number of other things, until I learned to fit the pieces together. Mainly I was fascinated by some of the names coming out of the speaker. For the Giants— Mel Ott, "Prince Hal" Schumacher, LeRoy "Tarzan" Parmelee, "Fat Freddie" Fitzsimmons. With the Senators there were names like Ossie Bluege, "Goose" Goslin, Heinie Manush, "General" Crowder. I suppose it was natural for those names to have a special appeal to a young child whose earliest recollections of names were those of Latin origin from my mother's Panamanian heritage or the lilt and cadence of my father's Jamaican background.

Before I knew the game, I knew the names. After I knew the names, I categorized them into teams and leagues. It was fun. I suppose something like a giant crossword puzzle. However, the whole thrust was my father. His enthusiasm was contagious.

My father was like that when he was young. He was fascinated and curious about everything. When he was in Jamaica, he was a cricket fanatic. My father left Jamaica when he was nineteen. He wanted to become a sea captain as his recently departed father had been. His father was Scottish and trained in Aberdeen. Since Ja-

11

maica was still a British colony, that was a privilege Blacks were denied. So he decided to come to the land of opportunity—America. The same conditions existed here, but somehow he still managed to fall in love with America. Baseball was one of his first attractions. Dick Reid, his brother-in-law, took him to the Polo Grounds to see the New York Giants play the St. Louis Cardinals. My father immediately fell in love with the Redbird uniforms and the likes of Sunny Jim Bottomley, Chick Hafey, Ray Blades, and Jesse Haines.

Uncle Johnny, "Uncle" Armando, my younger cousin Irving, and I would sometimes all take off for a day at the game. I really loved this. All day at home I was surrounded by my mother, Aunt Doris, Aunt Pet, Aunt Beryl, and loving, visiting "aunts." It was nice being spoiled by the ladies, but the baseball game provided the male camaraderie I cherished.

It was opening day at home for the New York Giants as they took on the Boston Braves. On this occasion, April 1935, my father and I were sitting in the right field grandstand at the Polo Grounds. It was snowing. I had on tan leather leggings, a navy blue pea coat, and an eton cap. It was Babe Ruth's last season in the major leagues. He was with the Boston Braves. Before that Ruth had had fifteen brilliant years with the New York Yankees and prior to that, six equally scintillating seasons with the Boston Red Sox. During the flag-raising ceremonies my father made a special point to say, "There he is, Babe Ruth—the Bambino . . . the Sultan of Swat." My father also pointed out some of the other Braves players: Shanty Hogan, Danny MacFayden, Pinky Whitney, and Fred Frankhouse. Then on the Giants he showed me Mel Ott, Dick Bartell, Travis Jackson, Carl Hubbell, Bill Terry, and Hank Leiber. Baseball, I loved it!

I clearly remember my first World Series game at the Polo Grounds between the Giants and the Yankees. It was a beautiful October Saturday in 1936. That morning my mother took me to Macy's to get a pair of Gro shoes. I remember discussing the upcoming game with the shoe salesman, Mr. Azarella. In those days you sort of had your regular salesperson. I don't know if it was just good salesmanship—or was he really that delighted talking to this skinny little Black kid who had for his age extensive knowledge about the sport?

The excitement at the Polo Grounds that afternoon for the second contest of the fall classic was something else. President Franklin Delano Roosevelt threw out the first ball. I remember the final score—the Yankees 18, the Giants 4. Tony Lazzeri of the Yankees hit a home run with the bases loaded to the opposite field. He hit it off of Giant right-hander Dick Coffman. That was a spectacle. Lefty Gomez was pitching that day for the Yankees. I can see him now stepping off the mound to watch an old prop plane fly over the Polo Grounds. How much drama can you ask for—the last out of the game—Hank Leiber, Giant center field, hit a prodigious wallop to deep center field right in the cinder tracks to Joe DiMaggio, who caught the ball between the two flights of stairs that led to the clubhouse dressing rooms.

Instead of running up the steps after he had made the catch, DiMaggio stood at the bottom of the stairs with his baseball cap over his heart while the president was being driven from the box seats behind the Giants dugout to the center field exit onto Eighth Avenue. As he passed DiMaggio, the president saluted Joe amid the cheers of all the fans in the Polo Grounds. Then DiMaggio disappeared into the clubhouse.

I recall that after that game I went home to 654 St. Nicholas Avenue; I went upstairs, got two gloves and a ball, and I went to get my best friend Sonny Curtis, next door at 656. For that moment I was New York Yankee right-hander Monte Pearson and Sonny was Yankee catcher Bill Dickey. We were just throwing the ball hard to one another, up and down St. Nicholas Avenue.

The turning point, the vortex of my life, occurred in April of 1937. The negative became the positive when I contracted scarlet fever. I don't know where it came from. Those were the days before innoculations and miracle drugs. I was in Miss Stebber's class at P.S. 186 at 145th Street between Amsterdam Avenue and Broadway. One of those majestic H-shaped schools. Anyway, that day I awakened with a tremendous headache. I told my mother I didn't feel well, but she is one of those ladies who feels that education comes first, and she told me I'd feel better later. Well, I didn't. After I came home for lunch—and it was one of the days we had chicken soup . . . which was every Monday—my mother felt my head and noted my eyes were watering. She called our family physician, Dr. James Whitaker. He examined me and said, "He's got scarlet fever."

For one month I was quarantined, locked up, isolated in my own room. Imagine a ten-year-old cut off from friends, family, my little sister, and my first cousin Irving, who was like my brother. All I saw was just my mother during the day and my father when he returned from work. I thank whatever powers may be for Marconi, who invented the radio. That's when it all happened. That sick period put the lid on the bottle and I would say redirected my life. I started listening to the Newark Bears ballgames on WNEW radio with announcers Earl Harper and Joe Hasel, sponsored by Peter Dolger Beer. That was a great Newark ball club. They won the International League Pennant by 25½ games over the Montreal Royals, and they had guys like Charlie "King Kong" Keller, Joe Gordon, Marius Russo, Atley Donald, and Buddy Rosar. They were really a minor league major league ball club. Probably could have beaten most of the American and National League teams at that time. The baseball bug hit me hard and heavy. It became my life. My entire existence.

The first day that Dr. Whitaker said I had recuperated enough to go out—guess what? My father took me to Yankee Stadium to see the Yankees play the Detroit Tigers. That day Irving "Bump" Hadley, Yankee right-hander, beaned Mickey Cochrane, the brilliant Tiger catcher, and almost killed him. Cochrane was in a coma and near death for ten days. Witnessing that made me aware that the game was more than a game. Funny how you can start philosophizing at the age of ten. Risks are a part of the game of life, and anything worth having is worth the risk. Two years later at the Polo Grounds, I saw Cincinnati Red right-hander Bucky Walters hit New York Giant shortstop Billy Jurges in the head with a pitched ball. With the spectre of Cochrane hovering about, I knew that something had to be done. Ironically, in 1941 Larry MacPhail, Brooklyn Dodger president, introduced the leather inserts, a precursor of the batting helmets we know today. This move was stimulated by the beaning of two of MacPhail's valuable chattels the previous year, namely Joe Medwick and Pee Wee Reese.

THE SHADOW OF THE POLO GROUNDS

Baseball! The game was my life. At one time I wanted to be a major league ballplayer, but I was Black, and playing in the Negro National League just did not appeal to me.

ROY COBB

Arthur was so crazy about baseball he was the first to reveal that a stickball bat could be likened to a pencil. You could hit spitballs with a pencil.

I remember Art had a bat he called "Betsy." It was a mop-stick. He accidentally dropped it down the sewer and he cried like hell.

SONNY CURTIS

Arthur was always emulating some hero. One year when the season was over, Arthur took to wearing a three-quarter-leather jacket and a brown leather aviator's cap. That winter I thought he was Eddie Rickenbacker.

ROY COBB

By the time the baseball season was in, we'd all have our summer shorts and Davega sneakers—they looked like high-topped space shoes.

SONNY CURTIS

We were all a very gregarious group of young boys with a common and, for those days, an affluent background. We didn't have a leader, but Arthur was the coach type.

I remember when I got hit by a pitched ball, I fell into a slump. Art undoubtedly was the most knowledgeable of us and certainly related more to the game. He decided he would get me out of my slump. I was to stand at one end of the street and the rest of the guys were going to throw baseballs at me. Well, you either got out of the slump or ran like hell. I wasn't running, so I got out of my slump.

ERNEST COBB

How well I remember Art and me playing outfield on St. Nicholas Avenue and dodging buses and cars as we chased the old Spalding. When we became young men, our interest turned to softball. We had one hell of a team.

RECOLLECTIONS OF A BASEBALL JUNKIE

LEON BOGUES

Our stickball team, the St. Nicholas Avenue Viscounts, were serious ballplayers. It was not "fun and games." I remember that Art wore a baseball cap daily. It was pulled down low on his forehead as if to shield his eyes from the sun.

When he played his position, he played in a crouch, knees bent, ready to field any ball hit to him. Art kept his eyes on the batter in a professional way. No smile, intense, he moved like a tiger at the ready.

Art read a lot and knew more than all of us. He was a kind of moving force.

You know when you get older, you look back at the foibles, the exuberance that pervades youth—despite the obvious disclaimers. In 1938, for the first time, I heard Walter Lanier "Red" Barber. Red was from Mississippi. Along with Mel Allen and Bob Elson, he did the play-by-play of the New York Yankees and Chicago Cubs World Series. Each of the three worked on a different network (all three carried it).

To me, Red Barber was the greatest baseball announcer that ever lived. I can still hear him bellowing from the radio speaker now, "The bases are F.O.B." (full of Brooklyns). "Dolf Camilli hits a Bedford Avenue blast" (home run).

When things got exciting, he'd yell, "Oh, Doctor." That corn-pone-talking guy could really call a ball game. He painted a picture. Through Red Barber I saw many a game on the radio. You'd have to be there when he described those epic Brooklyn Dodger/ St. Louis Cardinals ball games. Whitlow Wyatt versus Mort Cooper; Luke Hamlin against Howie Pollet.

I think of myself—a crazy little Black kid trying to talk and paint pictures like Red from Mississippi. Sometimes I'd sit in the farthest corner of the Polo Grounds, with no one around me, and actually do play-by-play, like Red Barber—a Black kid fantasizing. Red Barber made me want to paint the pictures. Now that I'm older, I'm so sorry that I was bereft of a greater variety of heroes.

I was becoming such a nut the manager of the local A & P store at 142nd Street and Eighth Avenue, run by whites, used to be driven crazy by me. Wheaties, the Breakfast of Champions, had pictures of ballplayers on the back of the boxes. I'd demand that he turn the boxes around with those long grocery tweezers. And as he did so, I'd say, "I've already got Mel Ott, Luke Appling," or "Wally Berger." In total exasperation, when my mother came in, he suggested that I should come in and help open the crates when they arrived with the next Wheaties shipment.

One small regret is that I never learned to swim, and except for my cousin Irving none of the other guys on St. Nicholas Avenue learned either. Who wanted to go to the beach or country when my St. Louis Cardinals were in or Georgie Vaz's Cincinnati Reds were at either the Polo Grounds or Ebbets Field? Going away was out of the question.

My mother, after demanding, anguishing, finally capitulated and went without me. She'd give me some money so I could buy assorted cans of what she called dog food. I had a passion for canned corned beef hash, spaghetti and meatballs. At the game we gorged on hot dogs and soda. I'm glad my folks didn't go away for longer lengths of time or I'm sure I would have died of malnutrition.

In the summer of 1938 I visited my aunt in Chicago. New York Yankee outfielder Jake Powell was being interviewed on WGN radio by Bob Elson. Elson asked Powell what he did in the off-season. Powell replied, "I'm a cop in Dayton, Ohio, and I get a lot of pleasure cracking niggers over the head." I remember feeling ill and a dreadful feeling of depression when I heard this. Powell was later fined and then suspended by the Yankee Ball Club.

That same year I vividly remember an incident that occurred outside the Polo Grounds after a New York Giant/Cleveland Indian exhibition game. Mel Harder, the Indian right-hander, hugged and greeted a Black friend of his outside the visiting team's clubhouse door. My impressions were varied. I said to myself, "Hell, if he can hug the Black guy outside, then why can't they play inside together?" I thought, America is a strange place. There seems to be some sort of love/hate thing going. But I was still too young to be able to discern these almost schizophrenic postures.

Youth is generally hopeful. I approached Harder for an autograph, and as he signed his name, I asked if he thought Black players would ever get into the major leagues. He gave me a strong, positive "Yes." When I got home, I told my father what Harder had said. My father laughed and said, "Very kind man. He was only being nice to you. It will never happen."

Ironically, in 1947, Larry Doby—the second Black in major league baseball—told me that when he joined the Indians that year, Mel Harder was in his last major league season as an active player. And more particularly, he was the nicest of anyone on the club to him.

Every Sunday I went to St. Charles Church at 141st Street between Seventh and Eighth Avenues, as demanded by my mother, and after mass returned home. But this particular Sunday, April 30, 1939, I wanted to go to the game at Yankee Stadium. My mother told me my dad was playing cricket in the field outside the Polo Grounds. Some friends of my mother's were visiting that day and my father had already escaped. After some desperate pleading on my part, my mother, in utter frustration, shouted, "If you want the money, get it from your father." So I did.

It was a gorgeous Sunday. The Yankees were playing a doubleheader against the Washington Senators. It was Lou Gehrig's last day as an active ballplayer, his body wracked with multiple sclerosis. Two days later, his name was taken out of the lineup in Detroit, thus ending his 2,130-game-consecutive streak. I was leaning over the right field bleacher wall because Washington outfielder Taft Wright was signing autographs. When I thought my turn had come, he said, "Get that scorecard out of my face, you little Black son of a bitch." He might as well have hit me across my back with a whip. No one, no one had ever spoken to me in such a fashion, and I had made visits with my family to the South.

It didn't let up—at the Polo Grounds a few weeks later, Cardinal left-hander Clyde Shoun called me a "Black bastard" when I requested an autograph.

Would you believe on that same day, St. Louis Cardinal right-hander Bill McGee rubbed my head for luck. Rather he attempted to. I knocked his hand off my head.

Yes, it was some bitter fruit I swallowed. Maybe I was stupid or stubborn or a combination of both. I decided no one would ever make me change my mind and in some way I'd get through to what I wanted out of life.

Such pleasant memories. Sonny Curti and I lived on Sugar Hill, where everyone said life was sweeter. Broad treelined streets, lovely, tall, capacious apartments, elevators, sometimes even a doorman. The sidewalks were sprayed down daily. When you walked into the lobby, you could smell the lemony wax that breathed from the wood trimmings.

Sugar Hill was where the "dichty" Blacks lived. A few blocks east was the Valley—to us that was Harlem. We unfortunately considered that only the poor and the underprivileged lived there. I realize now how cruel and snobby our attitudes were.

But Sonny and I loved to run up and down playing ball on our special turf from 141st Street to 145th Street. Across the street from the apartments at 141st Street was the St. James Episcopal Church, which included a tennis court, and four huge garages that extended almost to 145th Street. And it was in front of the garages that we played ball. The big guys played in front of Ace Garage, and Sonny and I could go up and watch them play and pray for the day we would become the big guys.

My friends—Sonny, Junior Manning, Georgie Vaz, Ernest Cobb, Roy Cobb, besides my cousin Irving Rust, Leon Bogues, Willie Edgehill, and I played in front of the Roxy Garage. We chalked in home plate and third base. First and second were sewer tops.

SONNY CURTIS

Everybody played stickball, or so it seemed. I loved the New York Yankees, and my heroes were Lou Gehrig and Joe Di-Maggio. Art was a St. Louis Cardinal fan. We had many a lively discussion.

Art was always serious about the game. I loved the game too, but I'd never seen a Black man playing and I didn't see any place in it for me; in fact, I wasn't even aware of the Negro National League until I was a teenager.

19

RECOLLECTIONS OF A BASEBALL JUNKIE

ERNEST COBB

As kids I remember Art and me going up to the Polo Grounds and after the game standing outside the clubhouse with our baseball cards asking the players for autographs. We were never refused.

I also remember as kids we kept scrapbooks of our favorite teams—Art had framed pictures of the St. Louis Cardinals hanging on the wall in his room, all autographed.

It was the spring of 1938. I was about ten when I started realizing the world was larger than a baseball field. There was a war going on in "Europe," which I didn't understand. Instead of my father and his friends talking sports and drinking scotch, they were drinking scotch and having heated arguments about a man named Hitler, oppression, racism, and inhumanity.

Somewhere around here Dad took me to my first Negro National League ball game. For the life of me, I can't remember the date. I think I was in a state of shock. In my entire life I had never seen so many Black people congregated in one place. After spending several innings observing this mass of gregarious, seemingly pleasant people, I started to observe the game. I had heard of the Negro National League but put no faith in them. Where could you read about them; where were those record books? If they were any good, why weren't they in the major leagues? Yes! The white man's voodoo had hoodooed me.

Dad took me to a few more games that started me thinking. I saw Leroy "Satchel" Paige, then with the Kansas City Monarchs, undoubtedly one of the greatest pitchers ever. Then there was the perfect catcher Josh Gibson and first baseman Buck Leonard, both of the Homestead Grays; Cool Papa Bell, outfielder with Pittsburgh Crawfords; and so many more.

I'm hanging over the bleachers wall in left field at the Polo Grounds in May 1938. I'm engaged in a conversation with pitcher Dizzy Dean, who has just been traded by the St. Louis Cardinals to the Chicago Cubs. I remember getting his autograph and then asking about Satchel Paige, who I'd seen pitch a week before in a Negro National League game at the Yanhkee Stadium.

It was very early; the gates had just opened—it seemed as if

Dizzy and I were the only ones in the ball park. I asked him whether he thought Satchel Paige could play major league baseball. Dizzy was a maverick, an intelligent, uneducated, brash, arrogant but extremely sensitive human being. He stared at me for a minute, and with his Arkansas drawl he said, "Boy, it's too bad I couldn't throw a bucket of calamine on Satch and make him white, because if he were, he'd raise hell in the majors." I then asked Dean if he would play ball with Negroes. He replied, "Hell, I play exhibition games against them. What's the difference?" Somehow that so-called crazy white man assuaged some of the terrible insults and taunts that I had suffered from my other heroes.

That summer I got a shock. My mother told me that my cousin Irving, my friend Junior Manning, and I were going to camp. I had a tantrum. The whole thing that had kept the winter going was the thought of playing stickball. I told my mother that summer camp was just across the street in front of the Roxy Garage.

Well, when we arrived at Camp Minisink, Port Jervis, New York, some seventy-five miles from New York, I was determined that I was not going to stay. There was a cross-section of Black boys from all over Harlem. They laughed because we had suitcases; they laughed because we had pajamas; they laughed because we wondered where to keep our toothbrushes. This was really rubbing salt into the wounds. I cried as I thought about Georgie, Sonny, Roy, Ernest—buddies. I wondered who was taking my beloved spot as outfielder—who would know the proper way to position one foot in the street and the other on the sidewalk. And, horror of horrors, my mother had prepaid one entire month—an entire month of my life!

Although most of the kids seemed happy, I wasn't until I found another wishful thinker. Walter Branch had a round, freckled face, and a devious look about him. We conferred and decided to plan our escape. It was almost one week from the day of our arrival. We went to bed with our clothes on. As soon as we thought everyone was asleep, we headed for the highway thinking that we could hitchhike back to New York.

Our roadside pitch lasted about fifteen minutes. The state troopers picked us up and carted us back to the camp. I called my mother—she would not relent. Sonny Curtis had gone to the camp the previous year; he had stayed only about ten days. Sonny was clever; he figured the only way he could get out of there was to go "ape." I think they were happy to see him go. My mother had heard that trick, and I knew it wouldn't work.

The only thing that saved me from total insanity was the night they had the Sports Quiz Contest. Needless to say, I wowed them. The other kids stopped laughing at me, and I was treated with some degree of awe. One day one of the campers and I were walking along and talking about sports, and a tall, gangly, dark brown man came over to me and said, "Little boy, do you know who I am?" I looked at him and said, "Sorry, sir, I don't." He said, "My name is John Henry 'Pop' Lloyd, the greatest shortstop that ever played baseball. Now don't you forget that name." I never did. I felt a sense of embarrassment about my ignorance and a deeper feeling of shame because of my lack of knowledge and respect of the Negro National League.

Somehow, sports got me through that summer, and I knew that there was a whole segment of baseball I had to learn about. I badgered all of my father's friends about Black baseball players.

ROY COBB

There was a guy named Chump who worked for the local Italian ice and numbers man. Chump was older than we were, but he loved baseball and called us kids his farm system—Roxy Garage Location. He was strictly a Joe DiMaggio fan, but Arthur got a lot of information out of him about the Negro National League. Arthur could be a nuisance about information.

My first physical encounter with Branch Rickey was in the spring of 1940. I was walking up Eighth Avenue to the Polo Grounds and just passing the parking lot that was right next door to the ballpark when I spotted Rickey getting out of a car with his wife or daughter, I can't recall which. With jaunty courage, I walked up to him with my little piece of paper and asked him to give me his autograph. By way of identification I said, "Mr. Rickey, my name is Arthur Rust, a St. Louis Cardinal fan, and do you think Negroes will ever play major league baseball?'' He smiled at me and very graciously signed my solitary piece of paper. Then he put his arm around me, with the sun glinting off his little round gold-rimmed glasses, and said, ''Young man, you will live to see Negroes playing major league baseball.'' When he said it, I thought to myself, it sounds good; he sounds sincere, but I don't think I'll ever live to see it.

But there were things going on that I didn't know about. Shirley Povich of the *Washington Post* and other intrepid writers began protesting the color bar in baseball.

Then along came Sunday December 7, 1941. Sonny Curtis, Irving, Junior Manning, and I were trying to decide what to do. I wanted to go to the baseball game to see the Giants and Dodgers. It was a cold day, and I was overruled. Instead, we went to the Dorset Theater on 147th Street and Broadway to see *Dr. Jekyll and Mr. Hyde,* starring Spencer Tracy, Ingrid Bergman, and Lana Turner. When we came out of the movies, a drunken man was standing on the corner shouting that the country was at war because the Japanese had attacked Pearl Harbor. I didn't know what Pearl Harbor was and what a profound effect the war was to have upon me and baseball, but I would soon see the changes.

Shortly after the American declaration of war, Baseball Commissioner Judge Kenesaw Mountain Landis wrote President Roosevelt inquiring about what the role of baseball should be during wartime. On January 15, 1942, the President responded in his now famous Green Light Letter. As he indicated, the President felt that baseball, as the national sports pastime, should not be restricted, as it would be a great morale builder for the American people. He did point out that eligible players would not be exempt from the draft and that older men would have to fill in the void.

I knew I didn't care who was playing so long as there was baseball. True, I knew too that the quality that had existed might be diminished but the game was the essential ingredient.

I thought back to March 8, 1941, when Hugh Mulcahy, pitcher for the Philadelphia Phillies, was the first major league ballplayer to be drafted. The war seemed so distant to me that I thought little about it. After December 7, though, I could feel the changes. A lot of the older guys who played stickball in front of the Ace Garage were being drafted or were volunteering for the Armed Services. That spring the Roxy Garage kids became the older guys, and we moved up to the Ace Garage.

Now that we were big-timers, we decided we should have baseball jackets. I suggested we should call ourselves the Viscounts and took charge of ordering the jackets. The only problem was I thought Viscounts was spelled Vicount. Oh, well, who knew the difference? That was about the time I was the first guy to get regular baseball spiked shoes. I had ordered them C.O.D. from the Riddell Sporting Goods Company in St. Louis. They came sooner than I had expected and my allowance was not quite enough. Thank God my Aunt Beryl was at home and that I was the apple of her eye. She gave me the balance, and I proudly strutted around in my Vicount jacket and spiked shoes. (I still have them in the back of my closet.) I needed those shoes for the hard ball we played in St. Nicholas Park, Van Cortlandt Park, and the tennis court part of one adjacent to St. James Church.

In the meantime, my beloved Sugar Hill was going through a number of changes. The quiet, nonrumpled atmosphere suddenly was intruded upon. The war was bringing more and more Blacks seeking jobs into New York. I began hearing different dialects of English that I had never encountered. Extra rooms were being rented out to total strangers who could pay the price. The congestion and what I considered an invasion of privacy was disconcerting (I was always a spoiled brat). Strange new kids hung around us older guys, obviously dying to get into a stickball game. Sorry to say, I think we could have been nicer. Occasionally we would let them play, and I got the surprise of my life. What I didn't realize was that these kids from the South played baseball all year-round. They had the advantage of the continuous warm climate, and they loved the game as much as we did. I remember a guy named Bubba Washington who told me about a team in Jacksonville, Florida, called the Redcaps. They were redcaps in the railroad station and played ball too. Later I was to learn that most of these porters were college graduates and fine athletes that the Depression and racism would not permit to enter the mainstream of Americana. Bubba mentioned names like "Skindown" Robinson,

24

"Preacher" Henry, and Albert Frasier. Bubba said these guys would put half of the white major leaguers to shame. I didn't know whether to believe Bubba or not, but it gave me pause.

Other guys told me about the minstrel shows that traveled throughout the South. The shows were a cover for the fine baseball that was being played. I guess that now you'd call them poverty-stricken entrepreneurs. The teams would drum up business in the morning by having parades and wearing outlandish costumes, but that afternoon they would have one hell of a baseball game with the majority of the Black population and a smattering of the white population attending—which proves that when you love the Game, you love the Game.

The minstrel shows covered the Southern circuit. I was told about the Florida Minstrels and the Georgia Minstrels. After parading all morning, they'd play the local team that afternoon. This was all a revelation to me. A local team of Blacks in the Deep South!! I had visions only of Black people picking cotton and singing spirituals. I certainly was impressed by the spirituals because every Sunday morning after Mass and while eating breakfast, my family listened to "Wings Over Jordan" on the radio. I thought the music was beautiful but remote from me. I was a New Yorker, descendant of a Caribbean and Panamanian background; I attended Mass every Sunday; I was, in my imaginary state, the greatest baseball outfielder that ever lived. Yet World War II brought different Blacks to my neighborhood, to my everyday existence, who enlightened and enhanced my life and who gave me a greater appreciation of my fondest love—baseball!

I remember a girl named Loretta. I think she was from Charleston, South Carolina. She was built like a tree stump. Her face was plain, but she had a look of determination and intelligence imprinted on that face. Loretta was a deep brown with sharp piercing eyes. Every day, when we were playing stickball, she'd stand off to the side with her obvious silent judgment. She'd just stand there with her neatly braided hair with bows, a "mammy-made" dress trimmed with lace, and sneakers. After a week or two she didn't ask but demanded to play. We older guys told her to shove off. Finally, one day, as a lark and because we had been doing so well, we said, "O.K., Loretta, you've got it."

We gave her the stick, and my cousin Irving started pitching. Damned if that little brown broad didn't clout that Spalding all the way down St. Nicholas Avenue. That was only the beginning. Loretta could do everything. Apparently in the South girls also were avid baseball fans and actively played the game. You have no idea what that little tree stump of a brown-skinned girl did to our male egos. All of us older guys were happy when her family found an apartment and moved to Brooklyn. I wonder what has become of her. She taught me some lessons that prepared me for the Women's Liberation Movement decades later.

The year 1943 was a totally confusing time for me. The world was upside-down. In order to conserve rail transport for military use, spring training for baseball was limited to locations east of the Mississippi and north of the Ohio River. I vividly remember newspaper pictures of Brooklyn Dodgers' Dolf Camilli, Arky Vaughan, and Luis Olmo working out surrounded by snow at Bear Mountain, New York. The White Sox set up camp at French Lick, Indiana. The Senators pitched camp at College Park, Maryland, and the Giants at Lakewood, New Jersey. It was funny looking at pictures of New York Giants' Dick Bartell and Mel Ott throwing snowballs in Lakewood.

Actually that was mild stuff compared to what my mother told me in August 1943. With a very determined look on her beautiful face, she informed my father, my sister, and me (all the aunts knew already) that we were moving to 510 West 144th Street. I thought I would lose my mind. My entire world was St. Nicholas Avenue between 141st and 145th streets. How could she do this? Well, it appeared the war again intervened in my life. The growing population of Harlem had split the seams of this little confined area that Blacks were allowed freely to exist in. Increased paychecks afforded the whites the opportunity to flee from the encroaching Blacks and escape to the newly developing suburbs. Those large, beautiful apartments across the great divide—Amsterdam Avenue—were now available to anyone who could pay the price. So Mrs. Una Rust selected a large apartment on a treelined street. The building had a courtyard with trees and plants. My father and I protested vehemently, and my mother told me I could remain on

St. Nicholas Avenue and play stickball as long as I paid my own rent. Well, that was the cutoff point.

Then I found out that Sonny Curtis was moving and my cousin Irving was moving to the same apartment building that my family was to reside in, and Leon Bogues was moving too. I guessed that I could survive away from my beloved sewer-top bases and the Ace and Roxy garages.

I thought the change in my life was so monumental, and at fifteen you often think that way. Nonetheless, I had a smattering of the subtle changes occurring in America through my love and research of baseball. A white sports columnist, Whitey Gruhler of the Atlantic City *Press Union,* began talking about the morality of prohibiting Blacks from the major leagues. He had extensively covered the Negro baseball leagues. He was talking about freedom and democracy (abstract words to me) and about Black boys and white boys fighting and dying together—so how come they couldn't play baseball together?

Then there was Wendell Smith, a black reporter for the *Pittsburgh Courier,* who was carrying on his own campaign. Wendell was a friend of my family's; we had met him at a relative's home in Philadelphia when my sister, Valerie, was visiting. He loved talking baseball with my father and later me. He personally told me he always thought the Senators might be the first to take a Black because Washington was about half Black then. Wendell figured if half the city boycotted the games at Griffith Stadium, the other half, all Black, would attend. Sounded like apple pie in the sky to me.

There was a lot of flack when Nat Low of the *Daily Worker,* a communist paper, interviewed and printed a story in which Leo Durocher said something to the effect that Black players were just as good as white ones. Well, that's when it hit the fan. Baseball Commissioner Landis gave Durocher holy hell and then issued a statement that he had never consciously excluded Blacks.

On the basis of that, our friend Wendell Smith sent out twenty-six letters to baseball owners and managers asking for their reaction. Only six answered. Three supported Landis, and the other three were vague. Clark Griffith, former New York Highlander manager, came up with another plan. Griffith suggested that the Negroes should hone themselves into finer shape and perhaps someday, someway, they could play against the major leaguers and prove if they really had the ability.

This really made me angry. How dare he! Prove you are good enough? It was such a put-down I became discouraged and bitter. Then, on top of this, my favorite paper, the *Sporting News,* turned out to be against the concept of Blacks entering the major leagues.

ROY COBB

From the time we could read, which of course was young, we spent every Thursday afternoon at Crosby's newsstand on 145th Street and St. Nicholas awaiting the arrival of the Sporting News.

J. G. Taylor Spink, editor and publisher of the *Sporting News,* insinuated his racist concepts by intimating that integration would destroy the Negro leagues (they were barely surviving at best) and that only those individuals who wished to cause trouble and dissension wanted integrated teams.

Maybe everything I had heard my family say and that my family's friends had said was true. Maybe this was a racist society we lived in. I didn't know, and yet I knew. Completely. I remembered an experience while vacationing at the home of Aunt Edith, my father's sister, in Roosevelt, Long Island. We were just about the only Black family for the summer there. I had my baseball glove and a bat. I found boys with baseball gloves and a bat and a ball. We hit it off right away. Their names were *Tommy* and *Joey* Malone, and they lived in what I considered this God-forsaken country that was quiet, tree infested, and stream laden. They were good guys. We played the Game as best we could. I appreciated their skills; they appreciated mine. We had fun! The problem arose when I went to visit them at home. They had certainly been to the home that my family and I occupied. They had been lemonaded and sufficiently cookied. Yet when I went to visit them, I was not invited into their home. I was told to wait outside and they would soon be with me. It was then that the voices that I had heard at 654

St. Nicholas Avenue began to sink in: "The white man always keep you down; the white man think you're some educated monkey"; "in this white man's country you never gonna get nowhere—but the Black man can't ever get nowhere in Africa; where the hell we gonna turn?"

Tommy and *Joey* made me mad. We started out competing on an equal basis. Now suddenly I was outside of the screened door and being told that I would not be permitted in.

I remembered all of that, and I saw what J. G. Taylor Spink was implying. By now, at fifteen, I said to myself, the hell with it all. I found something else—music. My cousin Vernon Cooper was drafted, and he left his magnificent collection of Duke Ellington records in my charge. I was completely bugged out—what have I been missing, running up and down St. Nicholas Avenue trying to hit home runs? Duke Ellington extended to Nat "King" Cole and all the great jazz kings. Then I made the greatest discovery of them all—girls. Oh! Oh! Oh! Beautiful, soft, round bodies, calves without muscles—just their budding and some developing bosoms made life different. The parties, the music, the kisses, and the generally unfulfilled promises made the memories of the Roxy and Ace garages fade a bit. But anyway I made the baseball team as an outfielder at George Washington High School.

In the meantime, there was a man named Branch Rickey, a white man. The same man with the glinting glasses who told me years before with what I considered a feeling of love that Negroes would play in major leagues someday soon.

Rickey was a different kind of human being. He was a Christian who believed in Christianity—an avowed man of God. He was a brilliant and an astute business man. It took me years and years and books and books to really understand this extraordinary man. A former teacher, a former lawyer (he barely practiced law), a baseball player, and a manager is just a crude outline of the man's life. It was Rickey who brought the St. Louis Cardinals from a second-division club to the World Champion Gas House Gang of Dizzy Dean, Frankie Frisch, and Pepper Martin. It was Rickey who started the farm system almost by himself. And it was Rickey who took on Baseball Commissioner Judge Kenesaw Mountain Landis—the absolute ruler over baseball. Yet he remained a man of God and refused to personally participate in any aspect of baseball on a Sunday—his mother would have never approved. By the same token he did nothing to ever attempt to prohibit Sunday games.

History always needs extraordinary, eccentric people to make changes. This extraordinary white man went looking for an extraordinary Black man to break the color code of the major leagues. This was not a random thought or something dreamed frivolously. Rickey's past experiences as a baseball college coach had for years made him cognizant of the racial climate of America. He had had one Black ballplayer on the Ohio Wesleyan team, Charley Thomas. Rickey was shocked by the treatment Thomas received when he took the team out of town.

A man of Rickey's moral concepts, sense of democracy, and business acumen could not ignore the Black problem that plagued America. He began to prepare himself for an inevitability his intelligence told him he could not deny. With dogged determination that was central to the nature of the man, he read extensively about slavery and Lincoln; he read Gunnar Myrdal's *An American Dilemma* and the writings of J. Saunders Redding (a Black historian at Hampton Institute); as well as whatever other literature he could find.

Armed with his researched convictions, his sense of Christianity, and his all-American capitalistic zeal, Rickey set out to put into motion the wheels that would provide America with the first modern Black American to enter major league baseball.

Meanwhile, World War II was still marching on. Monte Irvin, Luke Easter, and Roy Campanella, as well as a roster of other fine Black athletes, had been deferred from the military. Bill Veeck, Jr., a baseball executive, and "Doc" Young, sports editor of the Black newspaper the *Chicago Defender,* made an attempt to stock the all-white Philadelphia Phillies with Black ballplayers. The plan fell through when Commissioner Landis gave his resounding silent disapproval to the plan.

Rickey handled all of this in a circuitous manner. In 1942 he became president and general manager of the Brooklyn Dodgers.

The controlling interest in the Dodgers was held by the Brooklyn Trust Company. George V. McLaughlin was the president. Rickey approached him about the possibility of hiring a Black ballplayer for the team. McLaughlin did not object. Times were changing.

With this approval, Rickey announced he would like to establish a Black team to be called the Brooklyn Brown Dodgers. This announcement was really a ruse; its purpose was to enable his scouts to freely explore Black teams to find an appropriate black player to crash the walls of racism in the major leagues.

When I heard about the Brooklyn Brown Dodgers, I was angry. I was angry because I was tired of what I thought to be the perpetuation of segregation. I thought, another Black club making little money, receiving limited publicity, and run by a white man.

Little did I know that Rickey's top scouts had ferreted out a young man named Jackie Robinson. Of course, the other usual names came up—Satchel Paige, "Showboat" Thomas, Josh Gibson, and more, but they came too late to the fair.

Jackie Robinson was not a name that I was unfamiliar with— UCLA football, Army baseball and football—a total athlete, but I still disregarded the rising myth of the man. I knew that Robinson had been honorably discharged from the Army as a lieutenant after three years service because of bone chips in one of his ankles; I knew that he had joined the Kansas City Monarchs of the Negro National League. I was aware of the man, but I attached no special importance to him. Dumb me! Young me! So unaware of the social changes occurring in America and the courage and defiance of one man—Branch Rickey.

On October 23, 1945, Jackie Robinson was signed to play for the Brooklyn Dodger organization, and the starting point was with the farm club in Montreal, Canada. That news blew my mind completely. Here I was ready to enter college. I had abandoned all thoughts of entering baseball on a professional level. But still— here was this Black man, son of a sharecropper, who would possibly be in the major leagues.

Believe me, I thought, pondered, and almost cried. My thoughts were—they're going to kill him, emasculate him. No, if he survives the minor leagues, there is no way he can survive the southern-stocked major leagues. Although he was an outstanding player and highly revered by the Canadians, would America be ready for him in 1947?

LEON BOGUES

When I think of Jackie Robinson entering the major leagues, I think of joy, greatness, and what took you so long. Of course there was trepidation—the racial problem. My indignation mingled with the assuredness that Dixie Walker and some other whites would do everything within their power to dismantle the credibility of Jackie. But I revered the man, his life experiences and education. I knew he had the guts to perform well.

ERNEST COBB

To me, Jackie's entrance into baseball was both revolutionary and ironic. I was happy as hell to see it happen, but at the same time, I couldn't help but think of the Black talent that had not been recognized, men who were certainly no longer in their prime. Jackie's game, as superlative as it was, was not at its peak when he entered the majors. The irony was that Jackie's coming to the Dodgers sounded the death knell of the Black leagues.

JUNIOR MANNING

I changed from being just a baseball fan into being a Jackie Robinson fan. Oh God, I thought, all I wanted to do was play baseball, but now it's too late—too many other involvements.
As proud as I was, I was afraid for the man.

ROY COBB

I felt such a sense of pride. Here was someone near my generation who probably would become an American myth. I could identify with someone at last, but there was the fear of what might possibly happen to this brave young man. I feared that his team would not back him up physically and leave him for the wolves.

SONNY CURTIS

I felt proud but angry. I was a damned good player— why didn't I have the opportunity? I hoped to hell he could make it.

THE SHADOW OF THE POLO GROUNDS

IRVING RUST

I was really proud. Finally we received recognition. I knew we could play too.

Yes, Jackie made it. He put up with all the horrors of racism except lynching. I realized he was special. Something existed in the man that never existed in me. I would have ranted, raved, and called everybody bastards and sons of bitches and would have been the proper prey that we have usually been set up to be.

No! I have never been that noble and self-effacing. Not that Jackie was, but he had to maintain that posture for a period because he was aware that he was making history. I could never have been a Jackie Robinson. At that age I was too shallow to realize the better good that was being accomplished. The so-called role of Uncle Tom has never been easy. It required intelligence, the desire to survive, to learn, to mollify, assuage, and conquer!

No! I could never have been a Jackie Robinson.

ECCENTRICITY
AND
MYSTERY

Baseball is such a simple sport and at the same time very complex. I don't even know that we should call it a sport. It is an American institution and more lasting than some marriages, wars, Supreme Court decisions, and even major depressions. Baseball survives! This American idol, however, has had and will continue to have chinks in its armor—thank God! Who wants to live with perfection? I can love, revere, and respect baseball, but I can also laugh, cry, anguish, and question the myths and foibles of the game.

I love the silliness of it. I loved those old boozing, tobacco-chewing, cussing, carousing S.O.B.s. Oh, yes, I knew they were for the most part bigots, but still they were the most prevalent and probably the sorriest idols I had.

I remember rolling up a slice of Wonder bread and putting it in my left cheek, pretending I was chewing tobacco like the old Arkansas "Hummingbird" Lon Warneke, then with the St. Louis Cardinals.

Another thing I remember was the continuing argument between my father and his friends about the racial "purity" of George Herman "Babe" Ruth. The first time I saw the Babe was when I was just a little kid—as I mentioned before, opening day at the Polo Grounds, 1935. Then I saw him as a first-base coach with the Brooklyn Dodgers in 1938 at the Polo Grounds. Over the years I recall his rasping voice on the radio. The next time I saw him was in 1947 on Madison Avenue and Forty-ninth Street. Ruth was wearing his luxurious camel's hair coat and matching cap. I walked up to him wearing my awed expression and shouted, "Hi, Babe Ruth." He looked at me, surrendered a faint smile, and with that gravelly voice responded, "Hey, kid! How you doing?" He shook my hand and then he walked on. I was in a trance for days. After I finally settled down, I distinctly recalled that he looked like a lighter-hued replica of my Uncle Johnny. That broad face, large flattened nostrils, full lips—and I remembered the spindly legs that supported that massive body and thought that maybe my father's friends were right. Maybe the Babe was just a "high yallow" black guy. I didn't believe it, even though I wanted to. Ruth certainly wasn't acknowledging it. In fact he went out of his way to deny the almost constant harassment about his heritage that plagued him throughout his career.

Any opposing team could get his goat. The bench jockies had a field day with him. Bench jockies would yell from the dugout, "Hey, nigger, can't you play today?" "Say, nigger, what part of dark town you gonna be in tonight?" Stoically Ruth would respond with an amazing calm. "Listen, you guys, call me anything, but don't call me nigger."

Ty Cobb, Detroit Tiger outfielder and KKK member, refused to stay in a hunting lodge with Ruth when they went on a special trip together. Ty, the old racist, said he had never slept under the same roof with a "nigger" and he certainly wasn't going to do so at that time, especially not in his home state of Georgia.

When Ruth was playing winter games in the Caribbean, he berated the darker-complexioned players and called them niggers and incompetent. His biographers swear up and down that he was truly pure white, and perhaps they are correct. According to the writers he was born to an upper-poor-class family in Baltimore who owned a small restaurant catering to those of German descent. Because of the constant pressure of a mom and pop business, Ruth was out on his own at an early age. His frequent skirmishes with the law finally led his family to place him in St. Mary's Industrial School for Boys of the City of Baltimore, where he remained from 1902 until 1914 (with occasional visits home).

In later years Ruth was often labeled an orphan who was adopted by the Ruth family. This too remains part of the enigma of the man. As far as the adoption goes, he never said yes, but he also never said no.

On the other hand, I've heard another story about the Babe. There was a good friend of the family who knew Ruth. This friend was from Kingston, Jamaica—tall, slim, handsome, dapper, and for those times well educated. This man came to America to seek his fortune, and he too found that there was nothing important available for him. He had no intention of pushing clothing carts around the garment district, mopping floors, chauffeuring the rich, or doing anything he wouldn't do in his native land. So this charming, intelligent man became a numbers runner and relatively his own boss. In the West Indies they called it a lottery, and it was legal. In America it was illegal, and they called it the numbers game.

The irony of it was the nomenclature of illegality, but the responsibility and respect it accrued seems ludicrous in the light of what is happening today. In those pre- and post-Depression days, the numbers man was the alchemist who could possibly change pennies, nickels, and dimes into hundreds and thousands of dollars. A lot of money for Black folks. These number guys lived well and were excellent businessmen. Their secret was honesty of the first order. If you paid off promptly, you had the confidence of the community. If you were even smarter and paid back into the community some of your winnings, you had respect. Many a church and many families have been dependent upon the largesse of these special people of a special time.

So when this guy, my father's friend, tells me that he and Babe Ruth were friends, I have to believe that to the degree in which it was presented. This friend said that there was never any doubt in his mind that the Babe was Black. They drank together, played cards together on 136th Street between Fifth and Lenox avenues. The Babe was always visiting a good-looking Black woman on 136th Street. But again, I'll question it but not deny it. Harlem was in vogue in the late twenties, and it was the chic place to be, perhaps. However, this friend says that Ruth used to bring a little light-complexioned girl to stay with this Black woman on 136th

Street when he was out on the road. What does this mean? I don't know!

All of this was confirmed by another friend of my father's who bartended at the La Mar Cherie, an exclusive watering hole on Sugar Hill. I remember that on Sundays we ate an early dinner and my mother and father would get all dressed up and leave us kids with an "aunt." They went out for an early evening of music, drinks, and visiting with friends.

The bartender had told my father about the story when Charles Root, pitcher for the Chicago Cubs in the third game of the 1932 World Series, started yammering something at Ruth. At that point Ruth pointed to the stand, where he said he was going to hit the ball, and Ruth did it. The bartender said he was there, he spoke to Ruth later, and the latter told him that Root had called him a nigger. Babe was determined to fix him, and he did. Biographer Robert W. Creamer in the book *Babe* states, "Root said something from the mound, and Ruth said something back."

Again, who knows? When I really got into the sports scene as a professional adult, Dan Daniel, a respected reporter and baseball writer for the *World Telegram* who covered the Yankees from the time they were called the Highlanders, told me in 1952 at a Boxing Writers dinner that without a doubt Babe Ruth gave every evidence of having mixed blood, and unfortunately, in America, that means you're Black.

Babe Ruth was such an individualistic man that I still remember and laugh about his biting remarks. I continue to wonder if they came from pure honesty or tongue-in-cheek humor. There was a sincere vulgarity about Ruth that some people might find unacceptable, deplorable, or humorous. Once, when he attended a very fancy dinner, the hostess inquired if Ruth would like some asparagus. Ruth replied with great gentility, "No, thank you, ma'am, it makes my piss smell." Ruth used words like *pussy* and *cunt* as if they were a part of the general American vocabulary. But then who cares?—he could play the Game, and that's what he was being paid for.

The last time I saw the Babe was April 27, 1947. He had that damned cancer, and they gave him a day at Yankee Stadium. That afternoon Philadelphia Athletics right fielder Elmer Valo made one helluva catch off Yankee Tommy Henrich. He caught a drive, banged up against the wall, and knocked himself out. Athletic center fielder Sam Chapman ran over, pulled the ball out of the unconscious Valo's glove, and showed it to the umpire, who then gave the out sign.

I was there with my pop. Of course Ruth had on his trademark camel's hair coat and cap—but he supported himself with a cane. When I saw him, I immediately thought back to his robust days. I watched the thin, colorless man state thankfully how much he appreciated the support of fans and how much he loved baseball. I cried. I cried with him, for him, and for the things that might have been, or should have been.

He died on August 16, 1948, and they displayed his remains August 17 and 18 at Yankee Stadium. On the eighteenth I went to view the body. Again I cried. The stadium was so packed it was impossible to count the number attending. The estimated range was between 75,000 and 200,000. There was an eeriness about the whole thing. The silence of so many people, except for sounds of occasional sobs and moans, made it seem as if a great god had died. At that point I really didn't give a good damn whether he was white, Black, or a mix-up. The only thing I knew was that a great athlete was gone forever.

So many other things pull my heartstrings too. Take Brooklyn for an example. I'm a Manhattan guy, but still Brooklyn holds so many memories for me. I know about Park Slope, Bedford-Stuyvesant, Bensonhurst. I know about the "dese and dose" guys. And there is something else I remember. A lot of people from the Caribbean settled in Brooklyn. They liked the semisuburban atmosphere of it—houses, gardens, and cheaper rents than in Manhattan. There were many Sundays, under protest, that I was yanked away from my radio to visit "cousin" whoever or "aunt" who knows. Distinctly, I recall rice and peas cooked in coconut milk with curried chicken or simmered beef latticed with green peppers. If not that, souse—a saucy concoction of pigs' feet and ears chopped fine with the addition of paper-thin cucumber slices, lemon juice, and red-hot peppers. If you had asthma or tuberculosis, when you swallowed this—I promise you a definite cure.

Then there was the black fruitcake, fried plantain, eschevece fish (which usually had bones in it—which I hated), avocado salad, and watercress.

To me Brooklyn evokes warm feelings, good food, love, and Ebbets Field—home of the Brooklyn Dodgers—"Dem Bums."

"Dem Bums" of course had their own particular and ofttimes special or peculiar groupies. For instance take Hilda Chester. I think she lived at Ebbets Field. Everybody knew her. Hilda had this funny deep froglike voice, and she carried a cowbell that rang to her rasping siren call.

One day, from her center field bleacher position, she threw out a piece of paper and yodled, "Give this to Leo." Pete Reiser was en route to his position in center field, but paying obeyance to a dedicated fan, he picked up the note and stuffed it in his pocket. This is truly a funny thing because at the end of the inning Reiser gave Leo Durocher Hilda's note. Prior to that Reiser was seen talking to President Larry MacPhail, and of course Durocher assumed that the note had come from MacPhail. Dodger right-hander Whitlow Wyatt was pitching a great game that day. Then all of a sudden Leo marches out, pulls Wyatt out, brings in reliever Hugh Casey. Brooklyn won the game that day by the skin of their teeth.

Dorocher pitched a bitch and berated Reiser for handing him a note from MacPhail advising him to "Get Casey. Wyatt's losing it." When Reiser explained that the note was from Hilda, Leo nearly had a stroke. But then that's Brooklyn for you.

Brooklyn spawns exceptional people. Arthur Miller, Norman Mailer, Barbra Streisand, Mae West, Danny Kaye, and more. Phil Foster, the comedian who used to yell about other teams' winning pitchers, "Trade 'em to the Dodgers," or if they were lousy pitching on the Dodger team, he'd yell, "Trade 'em to the Giants."

Another lovable great eccentric of the Dodgers' was Jack Pierce, owner of Jack and Lottie's Restaurant in Brooklyn Heights. There was never a time when I attended a game at Ebbets Field that he was not there. However, his greatest passion narrowed down to third baseman Cookie Lavagetto. Pierce would buy ten box seats to accommodate a hydrogen tank, two boxes of balloons, a couple of bottles of scotch, and a large gray-and-blue banner with the word Cookie emblazoned upon it. He would spread his flag out over the top of the visitors' dugout. Then Pierce would begin his chant, yelling, "Cookie, Cookie, Cookie" while blowing up his balloons. Every time Lavagetto would get a base hit, score a run, or make an outstanding fielding play, Pierce would pop a balloon, jump up and down, and scream even louder, take a swig of scotch and offer those in the environs a celebratory swig as well.

Before I saw him for the first time, I could hear his screech just under the voice of Red Barber when listening to the radio. I loved it. I could hardly wait until my father took me to my first game at Ebbets Field. My dad had to reprimand me for laughing so hard and not watching the plays.

To add to the cacophony, an odd assortment of Brooklynites got together as a band. There were about six of them. They really couldn't play at all, but they made a joyful noise unto the Dodgers. When they first got together, they were constantly thrown out of the park, but the fans loved them so that they were finally given permanent seats (which they paid for) behind the Dodger dugout. When the Sym-Phony, or, as I thought as a kid, Seem-Phony, disagreed with the umpires, they played "Three Blind Mice," much to the aggravation of the umpires. If a member of the opposing team struck out, they would wait until he just sat down and hit a resounding bang.

I didn't expect to see the same kind of carnival atmosphere that I had witnessed at Negro league games. Yet here were whites wearing the same outlandish clothes and performing some of the same ridiculously lovable hijinks.

Another reason I always will be fond of the Brooklyn Dodgers is because of my mother. When my mother came to the United States from Colón, Panama, she met and married my father. She enjoyed married life and adored her children, but she didn't understand her husband's preoccupation with "this foolish game baseball." After getting tired of his constant talk about the game as well as the fact that soon he was taking her firstborn to games, she decided to learn what it was all about.

She read the newspapers, listened to the games, and asked questions. As soon as she had a working knowledge of baseball, she began to demand to attend. My mother enjoyed baseball, but this relatively quiet, proper lady became a rabid Dodger fan when

Jackie Robinson was signed up and she saw him play. She jumped up, screamed, yelled at umpires' decisions like a true fan.

Yes, the Brooklyn Dodgers were special, and I'll always miss them.

The baseball players themselves are as much a part of the screwball syndrome as their fans. Some of their antics seem to be a cross between the superstitions of a stage actor and the rituals of a voodoo practitioner. Just as most of us look for outer reasons for a success or failure, so do many ballplayers.

I heard about the time Al Simmons, outfielder then with the Philadelphia Athletics, went into a batting slump. For the life of him he could not decipher the reason why. Simmons became disoriented and depressed. One day he took a shower, and naked and soaking wet, he put on his baseball cap and stood in front of his locker as if worshiping some pagan idol. Everyone laughed at him, but the next day he got four hits and broke out of it. Thenceforth after every game he went through the same ablution and the donning of his cap. So awed were many of his teammates that they too began to follow the ritual. It must have been a hysterical sight to see all those pink bottoms facing their lockers wearing only baseball caps.

Another favorite story is about Giant catcher Frank "Shanty" Hogan. This rotund lovable man was known for his hitting ability and eating power. Shanty weighed 240 pounds. Manager John McGraw was impressed with his .333 hitting average in 1928. So McGraw, always the showman, took Hogan aside and told him if he could lose about 25 pounds, it could improve his talent and he would be able to run a little faster. McGraw put Hogan on a diet devoid of starches and sweets.

A month later he had gained more weight. At that point McGraw demanded to see all of Hogan's dinner checks, which the club paid for.

After a three-week road trip, Hogan submitted his dinner checks. McGraw scrutinized them and observed that they all denoted the consumption of lean meat, chicken, salads, fruits, and vegetables but Hogan was still increasing his girth. After calling the restaurants, McGraw found out that Hogan had made deals with the waitresses to write down two salads instead of the double order of mashed potatoes he really received, sherbet translated into ice cream sundaes, and stewed rhubarb meant rhubarb pie, etc., etc.

McGraw gave Hogan so much hell he finally succumbed and gained better control of his appetite.

Some of the players went through a food fantasy fetish. In 1966 Jim Palmer, two-time Cy Young-award-winning pitcher, had a breakfast of blueberry pancakes. He won that day. Thereafter, he had blueberry pancakes for the following three mornings and won. However, one morning he overslept and only had time for a quick steak. Of course he lost that game. Palmer divined that the blueberry pancakes held the source of power. The story hit the papers. The fans would yell to him from the stands, "Did you eat your pancakes?" Some even brought pancakes with them.

Pittsburgh Pirate catcher Al Lopez once ate kippered herring and eggs for breakfast—seventeen days in a row—because things were going well for his club at the time.

New York Giants' Carl Hubbell would never step on a foul line. He reminded me of my sister, Valerie, who would not step on a crack on the sidewalk, saying, "They're God's dishes, and you must not break them."

Baltimore pitcher Mike Cuellar never looked at home plate when he warmed up. He would just throw. Once, though, the catcher paused to talk to the umpire, and Mike, as superstition dictated, just threw the ball to the backstop without looking, and no one was behind the plate. It must have looked like total madness.

When Leo Durocher was in the third-base coach's box, he always rubbed out any chalk lines that encircled him. Definitely a man who refused to be penned.

Jackie Robinson would never get into his position in the batter's box until the catcher had positioned himself. Rather than walk behind the catcher, he always walked in front. Not a too-trusting sign.

Billy Williams of the Chicago Cubs, a great natural hitter, had a novel good-luck method for sharpening his batting eye. At least once a game, he'd play hit the spit! He'd walk toward home plate, expectorate, and swing his bat through it before it hit the ground.

Pitcher Luis Tiant used to wear strands of beads and a special loincloth that he wrapped around his waist under his uniform to ward off evil.

St. Louis Cardinal pitcher Joaquin Andujar has this ritual about getting a stick from the bat boy to clean out his spikes—whether it is muddy or not.

Cleveland Indian first sacker Mike Hargrove is better known as the "human rain delay" because of his home plate ritual: Step out, prop the Louisville slugger, rough up his left thumb with his right hand, tug one shirt sleeve, tug the other sleeve, tug one batting glove, tug the other glove. And this happens before every pitch!

Boston Red Sox Wade Boggs believes he captured the 1983 American League batting title by drawing strength from chicken— as prepared fifty different ways by his wife, Debbie.

Superstitions are very real to an athlete. And whatever they think makes them feel comfortable in their job, that is going to help them, they'll do it, no matter what others think.

One of the most outrageous characters in baseball was Charles Dillon "Casey" Stengel out of Kansas City, Missouri. There were alternate days when I thought he was a jerk, dumb, clever, had tongue-in-cheek humor. At any rate he was definitely a buffoon. His non sequitur responses to questions were printed in every newspaper. He had a James Joycean stream of consciousness speech pattern that diffused as it was, you somehow knew what he was talking about.

At the completion of the 1969 World Series, when the New York Mets defeated the Baltimore Orioles, I entered the victorious Mets' clubhouse. (I was a reporter for NBC-TV.) I went up to Casey and asked, "How did they do it?" (Mets.) He replied, "They were drinking vodka, vodka." For those unfamiliar with Stengalese that means, "They were flying." It had nothing to do with intoxication.

I remember attending the Polo Grounds in 1939. Stengel was manager of the Boston Bees. Although his team was losing, Stengel, in his left-handed way, told his team that he knew they were losing but he just wanted them to take a little longer to do so.

Casey decided he wanted the umpires to stop the game at dusk, especially since the Bees were losing. The umpires refused. So Stengel got a railroad lantern from somewhere and said, "Don't want no trains to run over me in this here darkness."

The next day it rained. I remember that game. Casey again wanted the umpires to stop the playing. Again the umpires refused. This time Casey came out of the dugout with umbrella, galoshes, and a raincoat.

That incident reminded me of the time my mother bought me a yellow slicker with a fisherman's hat. I was dying to wear it, but it wouldn't rain. In desperation I got my younger cousin Irving to put on the hat and I put on the coat and we got under the shower. But then I was only eight. I don't know about Stengel.

Once the fans became so incensed by the poor performance of the Brooklyn Dodger outfielder Stengel they started giving him the "bird" (riding and booing him). Casey caught a sparrow and secreted it under his cap. His last time up, Casey, in an exaggerated manner, doffed his cap, thus giving the fans "the bird."

Don't be disillusioned. I was not a great lover of Casey. In 1955, when Ellie Howard joined the Yankees, Casey was heard to remark, "Finally they give me a nigger, but they give me a nigger who can't run." Still, he will remain a legend.

But then time changes and moves on. The year 1978 was the first year that female reporters were allowed in the Yankee clubhouse. Lord knows the ladies had worked hard to gain this very simple advantage. There had been meetings after meetings, conferences after conferences concerning the rights of women reporters as opposed to those that any male reporter from Oshkosh or Timbuktu was privy to. The female reporters were smart, tough, and demanded what was deservedly theirs.

On the last day of the 1978 season, when the Yankees played the Cleveland Indians, the women reporters were to be admitted into the Yankee Clubhouse. Sparky Lyle, Yankee reliever, however, had a different conception of what was to transpire as a welcoming party. He had had a large pink iced cake prepared with a huge pink penis *erectus* adorning the center of the cake. He claimed he had posed for it. As each female reporter entered the clubhouse, Lyle, very politely, would offer her a "piece." The female reporters frowned or blushed, and some snickered. Lyle is one of those guys who took a long time to accept a necessary change, and no credit to him, he was one of many who intentionally exposed himself when the female reporters entered the dressing room.

Social mores are now in such a state of flux that it is difficult to concentrate on a center point around which we can develop and evolve a more livable relationship between males, females, Blacks, whites, etc.

I well recall my own foolish macho image. I met my wife, Edna, when she was a student at Hunter College. She was bright, pretty, curvy, and warm. She would often talk about things I could hardly understand. The coup d'état for me was when I took her to see a Giant-Cardinal game at the Polo Grounds. She definitely was not a baseball fan. I felt good instructing her. Then, after the first inning, she turned to me and said, "What's that rag on the field?" "What rag?" I replied. "Can't you see?" she replied. "That white rag." To myself I said, "Oh my God." Slowly I turned and with gleeful chauvinism I said, "Baby, that white rag is second base." I laughed myself silly. I no longer had to be intimidated by this twenty-year-old goddess. I knew something she didn't. The experience salved my male ego. Of course, she zapped me later with some other information that I had to learn to absorb. But it was many years before I recognized the beautiful relationship a man and woman could have if they were able to contribute to each other's development as human beings.

Men have not been unmindful of the fact that the presence of women at baseball games affects the ambiance of the games and the behavior, as well as addicting women to the sport who eventually would become paying customers and increase the coffers.

In 1883 the New York Gothams of the National League tried out the idea of admitting women on a free-admission basis when accompanied by a paying escort. This concept (a forerunner of Ladies' Day) was adopted on a regular basis in 1889 by the major leagues in Cincinnati.

Two years before, the New Orleans club admitted unaccompanied women one day a week. The protestations from males was overwhelming. That a woman's place is in the kitchen or in the bed resounded strongly enough to stop the practice. Men had to learn to accept the fact: the women are coming and will keep on coming.

On the other hand, women are going through their own experimentations and explorations. Take the case of the pretty young lady who somehow jumped aboard the Yankee bus and exposed her well-rounded derriere, produced a magic marker, and requested that the players present autograph her handsome rump. Well, I guess it beats signing a baseball! By the way, Billy Martin, manager, caught holy hell for that little serendipity.

In a more serious vein, we must consider the scandal that Mike Kekich and Fritz Peterson, both Yankee pitchers, suffered or enjoyed just before the 1973 season. Those two pitchers were close friends. Their wives and children were also close friends. Then, in the light of changing moralities, these close friends switched families. After the divorce, Suzanne Kekich married Peterson and brought along her two children and pets. Maybe because Mike Kekich felt the pressure of this unorthodox behavior a little more, he did not marry Marilyn Peterson but lived with her and her children by Fritz as well as their pets. Perhaps baseball does breed strange bedfellows.

Those peccadillos are nothing compared to the tragedies that have occurred because certain and probably special people have become celebrities.

In 1949 the Philadelphia Phillies were having their best season . . . they finished third—the first time since 1932 that they climbed out of second division. The fans were ecstatic. Business was booming, but it took first baseman Eddie Waitkus to take the cake in the notoriety division.

Waitkus received a note in his Chicago hotel room one warm night in June from a girl he did not know. Her name was Ruth Ann Steinhagen, and she requested that he call her regardless of the time. Waitkus was thirty years of age; the young lady was residing in the same hotel. Waitkus called, and the lady said that she had to see him and could not talk about what was on her mind on the telephone.

I'm sure it sounded like easy prey, and the mystery of it probably excited Waitkus. He went to her room and was admitted. She went to the closet, pulled out a .22-caliber rifle, and shot him in the chest. Then, quite calmly, she called the house physician. Waitkus was in critical condition for weeks. Ruth Ann Steinhagen was diagnosed as a schizophrenic. She was in love with this popular player and determined that since she probably could never have him, no one would. I'm glad that she was a poor shot, because Waitkus recovered, returned to his position, and was as good as he ever was.

Ruth Ann Steinhagen was probably truly insane. But stop and think about the slight madness we all have experienced, or believed, or sought as a kind of solace to our own inefficiencies: A hat or umbrella on the bed was bad luck; if you spill salt, throw some over your left shoulder; if you drop a knife, a strange man will visit; if you drop a fork, a woman will visit. Stuff and nonsense; there are more fearful things out there to worry about, and why don't we deal with them instead of forks and knives, umbrellas and hats?

Then I think about the use of people as another balm to our not completely evolved egos. Midgets have been used as good-luck charms. They used to rub the heads of Black people for luck. Bill "Bojangles" Robinson used to dance on the top of the dugout every time a Yankee hit a home run. How stupid! We have been to and walked on the moon, and our piloted computer machines have gone beyond this—yet don't put a hat on the bed.

As they say, "We've come a long way, baby, but we still have a long way to go."

BASEBALL,
GAMBLING, AND
POLITICS

When I was a kid, I was lucky. Older people were always considerate of me and my quest for information about baseball. Joe Grant, for instance, was a wonderful man. Mr. Grant lived on the ground floor of 654 St. Nicholas Avenue, and although he was older than my parents, they were all good friends. I can visualize him now—dark-skinned, round-faced, pug-nosed, short in stature, and balding. He worked for the Post Office as a carrier. In those days of the Great Depression, this was a highly honorable job, especially for a Black man, and Mr. Grant was treated with great respect. Summer, winter, spring, or fall, he always wore a vest and a bow tie, which I thought was very classy. He'd lean against the balustrade resting his tired back and spin baseball tales to me day in, day out. The Philadelphia Athletics was his team. My, how he admired pitcher Lefty Grove, one of the dominant hurlers in major league history. Joe Grant thought Mickey Cochrane was the greatest catcher that ever lived. And then there was Jimmie Foxx, Max Bishop, Al Simmons, and George Earnshaw. When I was between the ages of ten and I'd say almost fourteen, he took me to any number of games at the Yankee Stadium when the Philadelphia Athletics visited New York.

I thought the earth revolved around a baseball. In those tender young years, I thought baseball was the all-American game. It represented the "truths" of America—honesty, good sportsmanship, camaraderie, etc., etc., etc. Joe Grant would smile as I sputtered or regurgitated the ideals that were being imposed upon me in good ole P.S. 186. He told me that baseball was just a sport to be enjoyed on a summer afternoon but that there exists in many men the corrosion of greed. Betting, gambling, had eroded the game probably since its inception. First men banded together to play against each other, and that was a good competitive outlet. Then they formed teams to play against each other, and that's when the evil started. There were players who bet against their own team and pulled little tricks to make sure their club would not win so they could make more money.

Then the teams got bigger and the leagues formed and the betting got larger. A case in point was Hal Chase. This brilliant fielder with catlike grace and speed was at that time baseball's premier first baseman. Somehow he averaged twenty-six errors per season. Chase had a habit of letting the ball "get away." He also knew how to arrive at first base for a throw from another infielder a split second too late. Eventually word got around, and anyone could discern that this was a setup. It was known that Chase bet on games in which he participated.

But even before Chase and others of his ilk, there were the Louisville Four. In 1876 William A. Hulbert became president of the Chicago White Stockings of the National League. Hulbert was one of the founding fathers of the National League. He demanded greater and tighter organization of the game called baseball. As a result of his intensive preoccupation, a league constitution was drafted that called for a firm schedule of games and what might be called a morality code. Hulbert banned the sale of alcoholic beverages and forbade the betting booths.

By the same token, though, betting is a primitive involvement that all of society, North, South, East, and West, has experienced and still follows. Where I grew up, lots of people believed that dreams held portents of riches. If you dreamed of an elephant, play 609; if you dreamed of your father, play 738. There were, and I believe still are, dream books printed and sold at the newsstand to help you interpret your dreams for betting purposes. It is in one way as if you expect the supernatural to help you gain more without undo effort. On the other hand, you have the very clever ones who know that making the sign of the cross and shooting dice will not make you a winner except by accident. Some people make their own luck, and some of those people were baseball players.

I had read that Jim Devlin of the Louisville Grays had won 30 games in 1876. The Grays were a fantastic team and had finished fifth in an eight-team circuit in 1876. They had a 3½-game lead as they were terminating their eastern road trip. There were 12 remaining games, and they only had to win half of those to gain the pennant. With their power accruing and the certainty of the game, Devlin was easy prey to a gambler named McLeod.

Remember, baseball players were not paid very much money in those days. It might be a little bit immoral (like a little bit pregnant), but the Grays would still have the edge if you dropped a game or two. All that was needed to fill Devlin's wallet was to fix a game and send a telegram containing the word *sash*.

However, in order for Devlin to play the game "that way," he needed his cohorts. They turned out to be George Hall, first National League home run king; Bill Craver, shortstop, a genuine classic fielder, not much as a hitter; Al Nichols, the only member of the Louisville Four who was not a regular.

Things got heavy when Louisville dropped games to Boston and Hartford. It became more involved when it was noted that the Hartford team had been the favorite in the Hoboken betting pool. Finally Louisville vice-president Charles E. Chase saw the light. On October 30, 1877, the Louisville Four were expelled from major league baseball.

There were lots of "little" incidents that gave one pause.

Connie Mack, manager of the 1914 Philadelphia Athletics, swore to his dying day that his club, which lost *4 straight games* to the Boston Braves in the World Series, did throw the games.

Subsequently, Chief Bender, one of his pitching stalwarts, joined the Federal League in 1915. The great Eddie Collins, second baseman, was sold to the Chicago White Sox in 1915. What did that mean? No one has the right to make assumptions, but educated guesses can count for something.

But it goes on. The World Series of 1919 began in Cincinnati. It was to be a war between the White Sox and the Cincinnati Reds, the underdogs.

Baseball, the all-American game, had its roots in the pre–Civil War years. It was a newly founded acceptable sport played by the gentlemen of that era. There were no salaries; it was an amusement.

However, those other gentlemen who observed the game realized that this was a marvelous avenue for gambling. Turnabout is fair play, and as the betting increased, so did the need to win increase. To win meant cash and a better way of life. Those young men who were talented and hungry enough saw a way out of a life of drudgery through the game.

After all, it was only a game in those days, before big business boomed. To receive possibly $100 to slow up or lose a game was a monumental sum. About the time baseball became the national pastime, gamblers, the great con artists, saw their way to making easy dollars.

Bribery of the young, often poor, and at this time poorly paid ascending professional ballplayers was rampant. Baseball pools were formed with subsequent agents and subagents—and here we are dealing with hundreds of people. The concept of a lottery proved repugnant to many people; therefore police and political bribery were involved.

In 1917, when America entered World War I, the government closed the racetracks for the duration of the war. The professional gamblers needed an outlet to secure their income, and they turned to baseball. Those gamblers were great psychologists. They observed and weeded out the "weak sisters" and offered them more money than they had ever dreamed of as well as the luxurious comfort of willing and beautiful women. For some guy from a little mining town in Pennsylvania, it must have seemed that he had died and gone to heaven.

In light of the above, it is not difficult to understand the Black Sox scandal of 1919. Even before that John J. McGraw, New York Giant manager, suspected that Buck Herzog, second baseman in 1917, sold him out in the 1917 Giants/Chicago White Sox World Series. Herzog consistently played out of position for White

Sox hitters. McGraw never could prove it, and thus no charges were filed.

The Unholy Eight of the Black Sox's scandal were easily identifiable: ringleader Charles Arnold "Chick" Gandil, great hard-hitting first baseman; "Shoeless" Joe Jackson, fantastic natural hitter although a functional illiterate; George Buck Weaver, all-star player at either third base or shortstop; Ed Cicotte, a pitcher who won 28 games in 1917 and 29 in 1919; Claude "Lefty" Williams, a successful left-handed pitcher; Oscar "Happy" Felsch, a fast clever-fielding center fielder with a lifetime batting average of .290; Charles "Swede" Risberg, a shortstop with enormous range; and Fred McMullin, formerly a regular third baseman but used as a utility infielder in 1919.

For many years the popular concept was that gamblers had approached the Chicago ballplayers, but later it was learned that it was a player who made the first move. Chick Gandil contacted a gambler, Joseph "Sport" Sullivan, and informed him that some of the White Sox players were ready to do business.

Sullivan worked for gambler Arnold Rothstein, and while he was discussing the matter with Rothstein, Gandil talked to the players who he thought would be receptive to the "deal."

The vortex was pitcher Ed Cicotte, since he would be in the driver's seat. In other words, control so much of the play. At thirty-five years old, Cicotte, feared that each year might be his last and that he wouldn't be financially well off when his career ended.

With Cicotte in the fold, Gandil recruited Williams, Felsch, and Risberg as active conspirators. Reserve infielder Fred McMullin overheard Gandil and Risberg talking and demanded in. The fix was in.

Cicotte threw the first game all by himself. With the score at one apiece in the fourth inning, he quickly gave up five runs on a half dozen hits. Cincinnati went on to a 9–1 win.

In the second contest, Claude "Lefty" Williams, the pitcher who was known for his excellent control, walked three men in the fourth and gave up a triple in a 3-run inning for the Reds. The Reds won 4–2.

Dickie Kerr, who was not in on the fix, shut out Cincinnati 3–0 in the third game. Then Cicotte lost the next game 2-0. The two runs scored when he deflected a throw from the outfield away from catcher Ray Schalk. Cicotte was a fine fielding pitcher and to many this was a tip-off that something was wrong.

Chicago lost again in the fifth game, 5–0.

With Kerr on the mound, the White Sox won the sixth game in Cincinnati 5–4. The following day, Cicotte beat the Reds 4–1.

The next day in Chicago, the Reds downed the White Sox 10–5 and "won" the 1919 World Series five games to three.

What was the reasoning behind all this madness? Let's start with Charles A. Comiskey, the Old Roman, a first baseman and heavy as a tactician, who became a manager in 1883. After twelve years he was granted the Chicago franchise when the American League was formed. He was a successful man, and his team won the first American League pennant and later two others. Comiskey became wealthy, and with that attendant wealth he was able to buy a strong club. He bought Shoeless Joe Jackson from the Cleveland team for $65,000. Happy Felsch came cheap, only $12,000, still a hell of a lot of money in those days. In 1909 he rebuilt Comiskey Park to the tune of $500,000, which increased its seating capacity to 33,000.

Comiskey spent high money for players and the ballpark but reneged when it came to paying decent salaries. Ed Barrow, general manager of the Yankees at the height of their glory in the twenties and thirties, rated the White Sox of 1917 and 1919 as the greatest teams of all time.

I never could understand why Comiskey would underpay those great ballplayers. I suppose he was just a cheap son of a bitch. Cicotte was being paid $5,500 a year; Cincinnati Reds' Edd Roush got $10,000; Lefty Williams received $3,000, and Gandil and Felsh only got $4,000. Nearly comparable players Jake Daubert and Heinie Groh on the Cincinnati team respectively received $9,000 and $8,000.

There were other inequities as well. While on the road, Comiskey only gave his players $3 a day for food, while other teams were being paid $4 a day. Cicotte had been promised a $10,000 bonus if he won 30 games in 1917, but when Cicotte was nearing that goal he was benched—not fair.

All of this made the players ripe for corruption.

This scandal shocked the American people. Then a guy about 5'7" and soaking wet weighing in at about 125 pounds came along. He was Judge Kenesaw Mountain Landis (at any rate, you can't lose with a name like that). Landis was elected commissioner of baseball in November 1920. He was as tough, hard, and uncompromising as the granite Kennesaw Mountain in Georgia that he was named for.

The interesting thing is that the scandal of 1919 did not become general public knowledge until September 1920. By then more corruption had evolved. Signed confessions were submitted by Cicotte, Williams, and Jackson—but before their trial in civil court, somehow, someway, their confessions "disappeared." After that the confessees repudiated their story, and the case was thrown out of court.

Judge Kenesaw Mountain Landis said "that regardless of the verdict of juries, no player who throws a ball game, no player that undertakes or promises to throw a ball game, no player that sits in conference with a bunch of crooked players and gamblers where the ways and means of throwing a game are discussed and does not promptly tell his club about it will ever play professional baseball!"; thus Cicotte, Williams, Felsch, Jackson, Risberg, McMullin, Weaver, and Gandil were forced into an early retirement.

After the scandal the owners needed a man like Landis. The very title of judge gave him a Godlike aura. After all, baseball and jazz music, freedom of speech, religion was what America was about, hopefully. Landis was what was needed—a former federal judge, an American patriot, a whisky-drinking, tobacco-chewing, strictly law-and-order man. His philosophy was definitely an "off with his head" syndrome if there was suspicion that a ballplayer had any aspirations of making a quick buck by fouling the game.

Concomitantly, a brilliant star was reaching his apex—Babe Ruth. Despite the bulk and crudity of the man, he gave baseball, and thus America, a lift. I am convinced that there are special people for special times: Shirley Temple, Fred Astaire, Joe Louis. Possibly such special people are not perfect, but they project an image that shouts, "Hey, I'm here! Look at me, and perhaps follow." These people grasp your heart and spirit, and we need them. Well, the Babe was certainly one of them. Ruth, formerly of the Boston Red Sox, joined the New York Yankees in 1920. Immediately he started busting the ball out of the park.

Ruth hit 54 home runs in his first year with the Yankees. No one, but no one, had hit home runs like that. Ruth was bigger than life! He generated a feeling, a talent, a competency that shouted "maybe me too" to the general public.

At any rate, between Judge Landis and Babe Ruth there came about a restoration of a kind of faith in baseball and Americana. Landis with the law and Ruth with his credibility and skill.

With the Black Sox debacle still fresh in everyone's mind, another scandal erupted in major league baseball. On the eve of the 1924 World Series between the New York Giants and the Washington Senators, Commissioner Kenesaw Mountain Landis announced that Giants outfielder Jimmy O'Connell and coach Cozy Dolan had been placed on the ineligible list.

The reason for Landis's move was a report that O'Connell, of the league-leading New York Giants, had approached Philadelphia Phillies shortstop Heinie Sands and offered him $500 to "take it easy" in the final season series between the clubs. Sands reported the offer to his manager, Art Fletcher, who in turn informed National League president John A. Heydler.

A hearing was held that revealed that O'Connell had followed the directions of Giant coach Alvin "Cozy" Dolan. He also stated that three other Giant players, Frank Frisch, George "High Pockets" Kelly, and Ross Youngs, knew about the bribe offer.

After questioning all of the men, Landis banished Jimmy O'Connell and Cozy Dolan from major league baseball. It was just seventy-two hours before the initial contest of the 1924 fall classic, but Landis believed that his rapid decision ended the matter. Many, however, were convinced that there was more to the situation than met the eye and wanted to have Landis call off the Series and hold an investigation, by federal authorities if necessary. The judge refused.

BASEBALL, GAMBLING, AND POLITICS

Yet the corruption continued. On December 21, 1926, outfielder Ty Cobb of the Detroit Tigers and Tris Speaker, Cleveland Indian outfielder, were confronted by Commissioner Landis and accused of having taken part in a scandal that also went back to 1919. It made the headlines. The two were accused of arranging to fix a game between the Detroit Tigers and the Cleveland Indians played in Detroit on September 25, 1919.

A retired pitcher for the Boston Red Sox and Detroit Tigers, Hubert "Dutch" Leonard, said he met under the stands with Ty Cobb of Detroit and Tris Speaker and Joe Wood of Cleveland after the first game of the Series on September 24, 1919. Cleveland had already clinched second place in the American League, but Detroit was in a tug-of-war for third place with the Yankees and could use some help. According to Leonard, it was finally agreed upon that the Cleveland Indians would let the Detroit Tigers win the game the following day. With this all set, the players figured they might as well place a bet on a sure thing.

The game played the next day saw the Tigers winning 9–5 over the Indians. Dutch Leonard produced two letters, one written by Ty Cobb himself, the other by Joe Wood; both missives contained cut-and-dried evidence that there was indeed a conspiracy.

When Landis saw the letters, he wanted all four men banned from baseball. Wood and Leonard were already out of the game, but Landis knew that baseball could not withstand another Black Sox–type affair. He therefore suggested that Cobb and Speaker resign immediately.

Cobb then threatened a lawsuit in which he claimed he'd make revelations of many interesting things about organized baseball, namely false turnstile counts and book juggling by major league owners. Faced with this, Landis backed down and issued a statement "exonerating" Cobb and Speaker. Both players continued their diamond careers through the 1928 season.

My friend Joe Grant the postal worker told me these stories, but I couldn't believe them. I couldn't envision my Joe DiMaggio ever being involved in anything like that. I equated Joe D with the Lone Ranger—white hat, white suit, white steed, "Heigh ho, Silver, and away." Would he ever do a dastardly deed like throwing a game? Never! As far as I was concerned, the rest of the Yankee

61

club was a conglomeration of Tonto—faithful companion. Oh, boy, it's great to be eleven years old.

The irascible Hungarian Joseph Michael Medwick, with the St. Louis Cardinals and National League triple crown winner in 1937, would never compromise himself in a nefarious interlude.

New York Giants' Mel Ott, my watch-charm idol, the little guy with the exaggerated lift of his right leg before hitting the ball, would never do that either.

Hey, Joe Grant, you must be wrong—those were good guys out there. Say it isn't so. But reading, listening, instinct made me realize in future years that everything that Joe Grant, that little bald-headed guy, said was correct. It saddened me, but I never lost my zest because I knew—where there were bad guys, there were good guys and good guys always won just like in the overly prevalent cowboy movies.

There were so many things I had to learn about baseball, and my friend Joe Grant had a captive audience. Grant told me and it was later substantiated through my own research that in September 1879 Arthur Soden, owner of the Boston National League Club, suggested the first reserve clause, binding a player for his entire productive years to a particular club. Other owners agreed to respect each other's reserve clauses, and thus a plantation system of slave and master was instituted.

Of course, the objections and hostility became apparent when the players realized what they were bound to. This reserve clause prevented a player from vying for a better salary, perhaps in another club, because he was virtually immobilized and neutralized by the new system.

Then when I was older and attending Long Island University, Danny Gardella kept coming up. This man was making waves. Danny Gardella was from the Bronx and a rabid Giant fan. His punctured eardrum kept him out of the Army during World War II. The depletion of talent, not dismissing his, made him an easy contender for the major leagues. After a stint with the Jersey City Giants, he joined the parent New York Giants in 1944.

This offbeat and marvelous guy defied the system unaware. He'd walk into the team dining room during spring training in Florida without a jacket or tie—anathema. It was bad enough that he had had to accept an offer of $5,000 from the Giants when he knew his talents demanded more.

Early in the winter of 1945, Gardella had met Alfonso Pasquel. He was one of five fabulous brothers named Pasquel who organized the Mexican League and announced their intention of raiding big league rosters. Pasquel told Gardella that he'd make twice the money in the Mexican circuit. With the kind of feeling we all have at one time or other—mistreated, unappreciated—Gardella signed a contract with the Mexican League agent for one year—$8,000 plus a $5,000 bonus.

Gardella started by raising hell in Mexico, playing for Vera Cruz. He homered in a 12–5 victory over Mexico City. Not only was his financial acclaim recognized, but his popularity lured Brooklyn Dodger outfielder Luis Olmo, a holdout who accepted $40,000 to play in Mexico for three years; New York Giant infielder Nap Reyes; Catcher Mickey Owen of the Dodgers; and New York Giant pitchers Sal Maglie, Ace Adams, and Harry Feldman. Then Max Lanier and Freddy Martin, a pair of Cardinal hurlers, and Lou Klein, infielder of the same team, deserted the National League. Lanier had been counted on to pitch the Cardinals to a pennant, and at the time he left he had won 6 games without defeat.

To show how serious the situation was, Jorge Pasquel visited St. Louis with Mickey Owen and attempted to sign Stan Musial, offering him a cash advance of $65,000 and $130,000 for five years. Musial was overwhelmed by such a tempting offer but decided to stay with the Mound City Gang.

Of course the backlash from the major league owners became apparent—slaves seldom run away without being caught and punished. There was also a great deal of flack from the Mexicans. They highly resented the idea of foreigners coming into Mexico and earning more money than the Mexicans. While the money was good for the expatriot Americans, they had to contend with poor lighting systems during the games, horrendous bus travel, a different style of eating, as well as the vagaries of the water and the uncertainty of their potentiality as regular baseball stars. Fortunately or unfortunately, the Mexican League lasted only through the summer of the 1948 season.

Meanwhile in America the fat cat owners of baseball managed to become cohesive enough to condemn and damn the players who fled the operatives of baseball, and Commissioner Happy Chandler placed a five-year ban on all players who had absconded on their 1946 contract to play ball in Mexico. In addition, he added a three-year ban on those players who defied their reserve-clause status when they fled America to earn more money.

In October 1947 Danny Gardella took major league baseball to court to fight the five-year suspension plan. Gardella had had enough of Mexico, and when he decided to come home he was zapped with the unhappy zest of Happy Chandler. I love people who say, think, or intimate, "Who the hell do you think you're talking to," especially when you know your impact. Grown-up people do not like being taught a lesson like a schoolboy. I say yes, buck the system if you feel it does not service your means and those of the general public—and that was exactly what Gardella was saying.

Gardella's case argued that he was a professional ballplayer being denied his livelihood by a conspiracy purposely enforced upon him. Gardella bucked the system. On June 5, 1949, Happy Chandler had a change of heart and surprised the world of baseball by announcing an immediate amnesty for all the Mexican League jumpers.

In review, it sounds like the Vietnam situation. I often wonder if Gardella realized his impact—because he led the way for Curt Flood to set up an all-out war against the owners and the reserve-clause system.

Curt Flood was in my time. I did not have to read about him. I knew every nuance of him. He was just a quiet introspective but guarded man. On October 8, 1969, just as Curt was making preparations to depart for Copenhagen on vacation, he received a call from Jim Toomey, assistant to Bing Devine, general manager of the St. Louis Cardinals. Flood was told he had been traded to the Philadelphia Phillies, along with Tim McCarver, Joe Hoerner, and Byron Browne.

For twelve years Flood had worked hard for the Cardinals. His entire life revolved around the game and his life-style in St. Louis.

Like Rosa Parks, the woman who refused to give up her seat to a white man in Birmingham, Alabama, Flood said NO.

Then everything hit the fan. Flood filed suit against baseball, attacking its reserve clause. He challenged the legality of the standard baseball contract. The parrying started January 16, 1970, and in August Judge Irving Ben Cooper of the U.S. District Court in New York City stated that federal antitrust laws were not applicable to baseball.

Judge Cooper noted, in a forty-seven-page decision, that the effect of the reserve clause was to deny a player career freedom, but he was more impressed with management's argument that it was needed to maintain balanced competition and fan interest.

In April 1971 a three-judge U.S. Circuit Court of Appeals, and eventually the Supreme Court, upheld baseball's reserve rule and its exemption from antitrust laws.

After the decision just forget about Flood's career. At the age of thirty-two he left America and went to Copenhagen to open a bar. That was not really his game, so when the Washington Senators offered him $110,000 to return to baseball and America, he readily accepted. He played only 13 games; then he chucked it.

Although Flood's career was ruined, he shook the foundation— and the "slave" reserve clause which automatically binds a player to one team became a question of much controversy. How much power should anyone have over the will of another person? Shouldn't a ballplayer have the same right as a plumber? What we're talking about is the privilege of choice that is inherently ours and under the present American system justifiably so according to the concepts of the founding fathers.

Finally the day before Christmas Eve, 1975, an arbitrator ruled that players without a signed contract who had performed one season could and should become free agents and have the right to sell their services to the highest bidder.

There were two pitchers who immediately enjoyed the largesse of this opinion—Andy Messersmith of the Los Angeles Dodgers and Dave McNally of the Montreal Expos were now both free agents because both clubs had agreed to let them play a full season without being signed. This virtually voided the reserve clause.

I am sorry about Curt Flood, but because of his obstinacy ballplayers are free; they can make their deals, get paid what they deserve, and cut down, or rather eliminate, the corrosive effects of gambling.

Perhaps now we again have the all-American game.

OWNERS

To me baseball is Camelot, that mystical dream to which we all aspire. There are kings, queens, princes and princesses, dukes, and knights. Reinterpret in baseballese, owners, managers, coaches, and the knights of the diamond—the ballplayers.

The King Arthur has to be some particularly kind of strong individual who is endowed with great wealth and must protect his special turf. The knights protect the king's wealth with their power, and in turn the King Arthurs assure them of prosperity.

One of the kings in the Camelot of baseball is George M. Steinbrenner. He was born July 4, 1930, in the Cleveland suburb of Bay Village, Ohio. His father was a very wealthy man by way of the shipping business but a strict disciplinarian. George was refused an allowance and told to go out and make his own money. He entered Culver Military Academy in Indiana at the age of thirteen. Athletics was his meat—playing end in football and running hurdles in track was as significant to his life as stickball was to mine.

His zest for sports continued at Williams College in Massachusetts, where, surprisingly, he was an English major. George must have done almost everything there was to do at Williams—wrote a sports column for the school newspaper, was president of the Glee Club, composed his thesis on the heroines of Thomas Hardy novels, played halfback on the football team, and ran varsity low hurdles.

After college, George entered peacetime military duty as a general's aide. And after that, rather than enter the business world with his father, he coached high school football and basketball in Columbus. Later, in 1955, he became an assistant football coach under Lou Saban at Northwestern University. He served as backfield coach at Purdue University a little later.

In 1960 George's "playing" days were over—time to get down to business.

The family's shipping company was in trouble, and George had to join his father in an attempt to rescue the resources of the family. He did it. He was not going to let all that old money be lost. George and his father worked like hell with all kinds of negotiations and probably a kind of ruthlessness. They say that his business interests must net him unestimated millions.

Now George could go back and "play" some more.

In 1973 CBS's William Paley decided to sell the Yankees. He found a willing contender in Steinbrenner and thirteen limited partners. Of course George owns the lion's share, and that's when we got into a different ball game.

I've known of and known George Steinbrenner since the beginning of his ownership of the Yankees. He's a tough competitor, a hard-nosed businessman, sometimes devoid of sensitivity for people. Many people who work for him don't like him—but then who promised you a rose garden? Pay! Cash! Survival! So you manage to tolerate a condition that if you had money in this society, you would dismiss as lightly as a gnat landing on your forehead. But that's not the case, 'cause you don't have the money and Steinbrenner has and he doesn't give a damn.

Nevertheless there is something about George; he's another piece of granite. I like and respect his business acumen—but Lord knows, I wouldn't want to work for him.

I remember one time in Fort Lauderdale when I was being filmed in a promotional TV spot for WABC with Steinbrenner and Yankee manager Billy Martin. Steinbrenner was irritable. His hair kept falling onto his forehead—once, twice, three times. The cameras couldn't roll until he looked right. The makeup lady kept making trips in vain to correct the problem. Finally I offered him my Afro comb, and George and Billy fell down laughing. It was merely a fun thing and broke the tension, and we were able to pursue the filming.

Every time I do an interview with Steinbrenner—TV or radio, at the end he'll tell me, "You're a tough son of a bitch." I told him, "If I'd had the money you have—look out."

I have not yet discerned whether acquisitiveness is an inherent quality or a learned one. I know I want; I know that where I grew up on Sugar Hill everybody did too. Riches come to the very smart, very strong, very talented, the takers or the inheritors— most times.

Take for an example Helene Britton. At the age of thirty-two, through inheritance, she became president of the fledgling St. Louis Cardinals. She was smart, beautiful, and a militant votes-for-women disciple. I understand that she undertook the affairs of the St. Louis ball club with great flourish—they began calling it the petticoat rule.

In general, major league teams are owned by individuals (or groups) who have made their money in other areas. Chewing gum mogul William Wrigley had the Chicago Cubs; Danny Kaye, movie star and comedian, had a piece of the Seattle Mariners; Gene Autry, movie cowboy hero, became owner of the California Angels; insurance magnate Charlie Finley owned the Oakland As, etc., etc., etc.

This is all true, and it seems to be an axiom that wealth creates greater wealth, but there is always the exception to every rule.

Now let's think about the exceptions—the odd ones, the ones that change the world for good or bad. Leland S. (Larry) MacPhail was one of those guys. He was the kind of guy I loved. He did everything: college athlete, minor league executive, worked in a family bank, headed a department store, was a practicing lawyer; had been a Navy captain in World War I. He had the audacity to steal a car after the armistice and drive it into the Netherlands with the plan to kidnap Kaiser Wilhelm to take him to peace talks in

Paris. The plan failed, but the intent of it impressed me as a child—how ballsy can you get!

I suppose it was fortunate that the war ended, because MacPhail was hell-bent on making an impression on the planet—like Alexander, he almost cried because there were no more worlds to conquer.

He tried the automobile business in Columbus, Ohio—but to a man of his dreams, that was a foolish interruption in his ultimate search for power.

Baseball was his thing; he loved the game, and it could be a great power thrust. He was brought into baseball in 1930 operating the city's franchise in the American Association, the Columbus Red Birds, which was a St. Louis Cardinal farm club. He had no problem with success, and he was soon in the National League—Cincinnati and then Brooklyn.

From what I've read and heard, MacPhail was not an easy man. He was irascible, moody, quick tempered, but he brought a special quality to baseball that changed the structure of the game. Who says you have to love an innovator, though.

In 1935 MacPhail instituted the first night game in the major league's history. On May 24, in a contest between the Cincinnati Reds and the Philadelphia Phillies, night baseball began. It was such a prestigious occasion that President Franklin D. Roosevelt pushed the button in the White House that activated 632 lights in Cincinnati's Crosley Field. It seemingly was tantamount to the launching of a spacecraft.

I thanked Larry MacPhail when Sonny Curtis, my buddy, and I attended the first night game at the Polo Grounds in 1940 between the New York Giants and the Boston Bees.

It was awesome, unbelievable, like being in fairyland. Disney couldn't have done much more at that time. It is interesting to see the march of history through baseball's Spalding ball.

MacPhail, the dirty dog of baseball, was probably the first owner to take motion pictures of players in order for them to study and correct their faults.

He made a spectacle, or perhaps created a curious aura, out of baseball to hype the game in those pre-TV days. Jesse Owens, four gold medalist in Berlin at the 1936 Olympics, would do sprints and broad jumps in pregame festivities.

When MacPhail joined the Brooklyn Dodgers in 1938, he introduced night baseball there. It was a time when the Great Depression was running its course but tapering off because of the contemplation of a major war. In anticipation of the war the powers that be started hiring people to work in shipyards, aircraft factories, and other defense areas. Now, with more working capital, more people could attend baseball games in their leisure time. Leisure time often was at night, and what could be more pleasurable or American than a night at the games?

It worked. The bright lights of the night games helped release the tension of the impending war.

MacPhail really hit the jackpot in that inaugural contest under the lights when Cincinnati southpaw Johnny Vander Meer pitched his second consecutive no-hitter.

Then in 1939 MacPhail took another giant step and proclaimed that he was going to broadcast Dodger games on a regular basis. Prevailing at that time was a monumental fear of broadcasting games among the owners. They thought it would cut down on the attendance at games and lessen their revenue. Of course there had been broadcasts of games but on a sporadic basis, and that had generally been in Cincinnati when MacPhail was with the Reds. Only for World Series and All-Star games had there been broadcasting in New York City.

Smart cookie MacPhail intuitively knew home broadcasts could only stimulate the attendance because of increased interest.

When apprised of MacPhail's intentions about regular broadcasting, the owners of the Yankees and Giants had a fit. They had instituted a five-year ban on game broadcasts in New York.

To counteract this, MacPhail contracted a 50,000-watt station (WOR) and sought the services of the best announcer he could find. Again he hit the jackpot—Red Barber, who had worked for MacPhail in Cincinnati.

Red Barber, the man who was the inspiration of my life. Thanks again, Larry MacPhail.

After MacPhail set up broadcasting the Dodger games and lighting Ebbets Field for night games, he became president and general manager of the Yankees—after he, Dan Topping, and Del Webb bought the team, the stadium, and the farm system for $2.8 million on January 26, 1945.

Of course one of the first things Larry MacPhail did was to install lights atop Yankee Stadium in 1946. Again the man succeeded in increasing attendance—5,326,295 fans flocked to the stadium, and the Yankees made more than had been made by any combined group of teams.

A coal strike interfered with Larry by tying up the railroad, thus limiting the transportation of the Yankee team. Undaunted, Mac-Phail contracted with an airline for a 44-passenger airplane to transport his team. This was another first. Soon after, most major league teams were transported by air.

In 1946 he sold the first commercial television rights for baseball.

The man was a giant!

Then there was another man who deserves his place in the sun. W. A. "Gus" Greenlee. Greenlee was born in Marion, North Carolina, and migrated to Pittsburgh, Pennsylvania, after serving overseas in World War I. My father introduced me to him with great pride at Yankee Stadium in 1937 at a Negro National League game.

I was a kid and much more impressed with Greenlee's boxing stable in which John Henry Lewis, the light heavyweight champion, was the star.

I was impressed with Greenlee because he had power and he was a Black man. Greenlee did not get his power through an inheritance. He got it through intelligence and the consequent strength that often accompanies it. He operated a bar—the Crawford Grill in Pittsburgh—that was camouflage for his numbers business. No doubt about it. He was the numbers king there. Gus even controlled a faction of political power in Pittsburgh. He was a cigar-chomping, light-complexioned, freckle-faced man of robust build. He was called Big Red, and he loved baseball, he had organizational genius, and he could easily afford to pay for a Black franchise—the Pittsburgh Crawfords.

Greenlee was not the first to foster Blacks in the Negro league, but I think he was probably the best. He had the money. Since Blacks were not to enter modern major league baseball until the advent of Jackie Robinson and since Blacks loved baseball as much as anyone, they formed their own teams and leagues.

The first Negro National League was founded by Rube Foster in 1920. It lasted until 1932.

Gus Greenlee put together the second Negro National League in 1933. The league opened with the Crawfords, the Homestead Grays, Robert A. Coles's American Giants of Chicago, the Indianapolis ABC's, the Detroit Stars, and the Columbus Blue Birds.

Like any enterprising entrepreneur, Greenlee stocked his club with the best Black players around—Satchel Paige, Oscar Charleston, Josh Gibson, Jimmie Crutchfield, Ted Page, Judy Johnson, and Leroy Matlock and Buck Leonard.

Black teams could use the major league ballparks when the white clubs were on the road but were refused use of shower and toilet facilities. Who the hell wants to run around dirty and smelly as well as having to urinate in a park? Greenlee thought too highly of his players for that, and with $100,000 of his numbers money he decided to build Greenlee Field in Pittsburgh. It incorporated all the facilities that are necessary for a team to play like decent human beings.

Black teams did not have the wherewithall to travel as "luxuriously" as the major league white teams—a beat-up car or two was the best they could do. But Greenlee had too great a respect for his players, and in 1935 he bought a GM special bus that was the most accommodating and flashiest team bus of the thirties.

Greenlee made an incredible contribution toward the advancement of Black baseball and was the creator of the East-West game. All the Black super-stars were involved in this particular production. There were 20,000 in attendance for this event in 1933, and by 1943 there were 51,723 in attendance. The games were at Cominskey Park, Chicago—home of the White Sox.

On these particular occasions, even the white press came out full force to record the magnificent display of Black talent. The revenue from the East-West All-Star game helped many a club to remain operative during those trying days of the Great Depression, and well-earned money could remain fluid within the segregated Black community.

Gus Greenlee was without question the number-one innovator in Black baseball.

Although Greenlee was leader of the pack, he was surrounded and supported by power, the biggest, toughest Black gangsters around: Alex Pompez, one of the illustrious kings of the Harlem numbers racket in the mid-thirties, owned the New York Cubans. (Pompez was forced to disappear from Harlem in 1937 when District Attorney Thomas Dewey attempted to arrest him. Pompez sought asylum in Mexico.)

When I was a kid, Alex Pompez was a friend of a good friend and neighbor of my family's, Joseph Casanova.

Ed "Soldier Boy" Sembler had the New York Black Yankees; Tom Wilson the Baltimore Elite Giants; numbers baron Abe Manley had the Newark Eagles; Ed Bolden the Philadelphia Stars; Rufus Jackson was in control of the Homestead Grays.

Tough cookies all, but they had the power and gave the impetus for the Black baseball league to more than survive.

Then there was another phenomenon—Effa Manley. She was born in Philadelphia in the early 1900s. Her racial background is questionable. She was the illegitimate offspring of a family with mulatto siblings. Her mother was a white German, but she married a Black man and had had four children before Effa was born. After Effa her mother married another Black man and had two children with him.

Identification is so difficult to pinpoint in this basically racist society we live in that whether Effa was really white or Black seems ludicrous. After all, being Black is also a state of mind, and apparently Effa thought so too.

But one of the most important things about Effa is that she loved baseball, and she happened to meet Abe Manley at the 1932 World Series between the New York Yankees and the Chicago Cubs. Abe was a hustler-gangster, Black, twenty years her senior, and a maniacal baseball fanatic.

Effa and Cap, as Abe was generally called, married shortly after meeting, and with their combined baseball acumen they set out to build a successful Negro National League franchise in Newark. They made a good team. Abe Manley could spot the talent of a player in a minute or two, but Effa was the one to run the show.

Effa handled the business part and the public relations for the Newark Eagles. Beyond that she was the treasurer of the New Jersey NAACP and fought for integration. As a charter member of the Citizens League for Fair Play, she worked hard with a group to desegregate store employment practices in Harlem.

I know all about this because my mother-in-law was part of that group. Edna Hayes Morgan has told me, perhaps too many times, that when my wife was a toddler she put little Edna on a sled a day or so after a heavy snow and walked, pulled, dragged her to 125th Street from 148th Street and St. Nicholas Avenue, to walk in a demonstration to protest the unfair hiring practices that existed there. Although my mother-in-law was following the exhortations of the Harlem Labor Union, Mrs. Manley was also part of that stew.

Interestingly, Kress five-and-ten-cent store refused to respond to the dictates of the Black people who were supporting and consequently providing the income for the all-white employees. Kress closed shop before they gave in to the demands of the Black demonstrators. Eventually the other stores capitulated, and at last Blacks could find jobs in their own neighborhood.

In 1946 when Jackie Robinson entered the major leagues, the Negro Leagues were in trouble. Despite Jackie's negative acceptance, the white scouts started looting the Black leagues. Attendance at the Black league games dropped so dramatically that by 1947 and 1948 they were virtually out of business.

However, the Manleys were probably proud that they had spawned the careers of Monte Irvin, Larry Doby, and Don Newcombe and led them to the majors. But all that the Manleys were paid for Monte's contract was $5,000 and $15,000 for Doby, and they received nothing for Newcombe. Effa was quite vocal in her protestations about the raiding of the Black leagues, but I say times change, but thank God for an Effa Manley.

I personally have nothing against the women's liberation movement; besides that, my wife wouldn't let me.

I've read about another woman of monumental power in baseball and her name was Helene Schuyler Britton. I hear she was beautiful and rich. Helene's father, Frank De Haas Robison, and her uncle Matthew Stanley Robison were the biggest traction magnates of their time.

The brothers also owned the Cleveland Spiders, a National League franchise. They were the true American entrepreneurs. Again they went about setting up their St. Louis scheme in like fashion, and they found St. Louis to their liking and concentrated here. In 1898 the team was moved almost intact to St. Louis. The team name was changed from the Spiders to the Cardinals, and now their uniforms were trimmed in red.

Helene's father, Frank, who was then president of the Cardinals, died in 1905. Then ownership passed to Helene's uncle Matthew Stanley Robison. Matthew died of blood poisoning on March 27, 1911.

The burden fell on Helene. The estate estimated in 1911 was $400,000—a formidable amount at the time. Helene, at age thirty-two and in 1911, became an active, vocal, and responsible leader in the assumption of ownership.

Although she delegated the voting to her representative, she attended all of the league annual meetings. Dressed to kill, when she attended meetings, she asked penetrating questions. Helene listened to answers with the tenacity of a bulldog and submitted her sharp, piercing rejoinders. You didn't fool around with Helene Schuyler Britton. She let you have it full force.

Times were not yet ready for a woman to assume this position, especially according to her field manager, Roger Bresnahan, who did not want a woman interferin' in his business, despite the fact that she "owned" him. She fired him at the end of the 1912 season (dreams of glory for feminists).

In 1914 Helene Britton assumed the title of president of the St. Louis Cardinals and as such was the first woman to hold that title in the history of baseball.

Maybe she was great, maybe she was not—but she did it.

Once long ago my wife and I attended a party given by Miles Davis, the great trumpet innovator and his then wife Frances Taylor, who was working as a dancer in the *West Side Story* play musical. Carmen McRae, one of my favorite singers, was there; Milt "Bags" Jackson of the Modern Jazz Quartet; Sugar Ray Robinson; and countless other big-time entertainers. As the evening wore on, all the theater people were getting up and doing their thing. Gerry Mulligan, the jazz baritone saxophonist, was accompanying everyone at the piano. For some strange reason, my wife got up, proceeded to the piano, and asked Mulligan to play "One for the Road"—and then had the audacity to start singing in the midst of this crowd of professionals. Edna is tone-deaf, and I nearly died. Finally she managed to finish. Gerry Mulligan said, "Baby, you can't sing, but if you want to express yourself, more power to you."

I'm not trying to make this any kind of put-down of women or the women's liberation movement. Thinking back, I consider my wife's movements at the Miles Davis party as saying, "Hey, me too"—and isn't that what it's all about?

I love those great women who achieve acclaim, and I love those great women who scrubbed and rubbed and saved their pennies to send a son or a daughter through college so that they could do better. Just as Gerry Mulligan said, "If you want to express yourself, more power to you."

Mavericks, mavericks, it seems that baseball is and was composed of them—thank God. It is the essential difference that makes you important and productive to the general society. Here's another one coming up—William Veeck, Jr. Veeck was the first who thought to purchase the Philadelphia Phillies from Gerry Nugent and stock the club with Black players in 1944. World War II was in full bloom. The Phillies was a deteriorating organization—what the hell, let the niggers in. Veeck was a nice guy and told baseball Commissioner Landis about his proposal. Landis listened politely without physically revealing his reaction.

But the sly old fox Landis apparently was operative in another sphere. Veeck returned to Philadelphia, thinking that he had the Phillies under control and could pursue his venture with the installation of Black ballplayers. But before he could pursue his madcap scheme, Philadelphia owner Gerry Nugent turned the franchise over to the National League. In turn, league president Ford Frick sold the franchise to a lumber magnate, William Cox, for half the price Veeck was willing to pay. Racial purity must be preserved!?

The 1944 Phillies, with Fat Freddie Fitzsimmons at the helm, had Tony Lupien at first base. Yeah! But Black Buck Leonard, whom Veeck had planned to sign, was a far, far superior initial sacker. Comparing the two would be like comparing a log cabin to Buckingham Palace.

The Phillies catchers, Bob Finley, Johnny Peacock, and Andy Seminick, couldn't play in the same park with the great Black backstopper Josh Gibson. Pitching, they had nothing like a Satchel Paige or a Dan Bankhead.

The bowlegged Ray Dandridge was to be the third baseman on Veeck's team. Dandridge was the best hot corner guy—white or Black—in any league.

At third base the Phillies had a nonentity named Glen Stewart.

These Black guys would have moved the last place Philadelphia club to a possible pennant and championship.

Veeck's father, William Veeck, Sr., was president of the Chicago Cubs in 1917 when little Bill was only three. Bill Veeck, Jr., entered baseball wearing a mantle.

Bill Veeck was outrageous, a showman, a con man, whatever, and his scenario worked. In 1951 on August 18, when Veeck was general manager of the St. Louis Browns, during the second game of a doubleheader against the Detroit Tigers, Bill Veeck sent a twenty-six-year-old 43″-tall man named Edward Gaedel to the plate to pinch-hit for Brown center fielder Frank Saucier. Saucier was probably the only major league ballplayer to be taken out for a midget.

Expecting repercussions, Veeck sent manager Zack Taylor to home plate with a copy of the midget's contract. Will Harridge, president of the American League, was infuriated and grabbed the phone in an attempt to keep Gaedel from batting, but clever Veeck had been anticipating this and took the phone off the hook and closed down the teletype machine.

It was a good promotion trick, but should we take advantage of the human beings who are odd and different? Should we hate or adulate them? I say no. Everyone is due a place in the sun. But the midget Eddie Gaedel's name is down in history.

American League president Will Harridge forbade the use of Eddie Gaedel; I learned about another kind of discrimination.

When I was a kid, during the Great Depression, the movie houses seduced and induced you to spend your few pennies to enter their emporium by giving you free glassware, dinnerware, or certain precious items.

My mother-in-law had the lucky ticket to win a squirrel fur jacket at the Washington movie house on 150th Street and Amsterdam Avenue. When her number was called, she ran up to the stage to collect her prize, and the crowd booed. I suppose it was because she was already wearing a silver fox jacket.

Veeck also enticed the fans with tempting offers—a swaybacked horse, a hundred-pound cake of ice, three live pigeons. When his team scored or did something spectacular, the scoreboards would explode like cannons were inside of them. Perhaps he should have worked for Barnum and Bailey.

CHAPTER

V

MANAGERS AND COACHES

Managers are a different breed. They have to *do*. One of my favorites was Leo Durocher. He was one of the most colorful figures. Durocher had played with the New York Yankees of the 1920s and won fame as the shortstop with Branch Rickey's Gas House Gang in St. Louis and the Brooklyn Dodgers during the 1930s. Durocher was never a good hitter, but he was a brilliant glove man, and as a hard-nosed, aggressive competitor he was aces.

I loved him; he had style. Off the field he was a sharp dresser (they nicknamed him Fifth Avenue) and mixed with the stars of Hollywood and Broadway as well as some of the unsavory sort who naturally follow in the wake of celebrities.

With a first-rate mind Durocher had the intuitive knowledge to motivate players and almost summon fans to the ballpark.

There was a good friend of the family, Richard Ball; he was studying to be a lawyer, and I had the sneaking feeling that he liked my Aunt Doris. But to me the important thing about Richard Ball was that he taught me a lot about baseball. He and Durocher grew up together in West Springfield, Massachusetts.

It seems almost ironic that so many people who influenced my life were surrounded by baseball.

*   *   *

Leo Durocher's management career began with the Brooklyn Dodgers in 1939. He was another one of those tough cookies. The stuff that "stuff" is made from.

Leo was one of the finest baseball tacticians I ever saw, and he never did things by the book. In 1937, the first time I saw him, he was with my favorite club, the St. Louis Cardinals. I saw him exiting the visiting team's clubhouse door on Eighth Avenue at the Polo Grounds, and I noted how magnificently he was dressed. Later I found out that he was the first recorded Yankee to appear in a Florida hotel lobby during spring training in formal dinner clothes.

Definitely my kind of guy. He had class, Charlie.

But more important to me was his stand regarding the hiring of Jackie Robinson when he was manager of the Dodgers. The players balked at the concept of Jackie coming into the club because he was Black.

Leo pondered about it, not in terms of his racial convictions but more directly in terms of dealing with a team who had hostile feelings about the first Black to enter the modern major leagues. The players drew up a petition protesting the admittance of Robinson. Now a manager had to manage, and Durocher did that as precisely as a captain runs a ship.

One of the chief protagonists was Dixie Walker. He was the one who was going to present Branch Rickey with the petition.

The Dodger club was in Panama to compete against the Caribbean All-Stars. The Montreal club had Jackie Robinson, and as well Roy Campanella, Don Newcombe, and Roy Partlow attending. While the Dodgers stayed at Fort Gulick, the U.S. barracks, the Montreal players set up on the other side of the isthmus.

The entire situation could divide the team and destroy the effectiveness of the club. In the middle of the night, wearing his pajamas, Durocher summoned everybody to meet in an empty kitchen. He told them that if there was anyone who didn't want to play with Robinson, that that was just too bad. Leo warned Dixie Walker that if he presented Branch Rickey with a letter asking to be traded, that his request would be granted. And as for the petition, the players could "wipe their ass" with it.

He let them know he wanted team play, and Leo didn't care with whom they had to work. Durocher let them know that Robinson was a great ballplayer and would make money for all of them. Tough customer, Leo Durocher.

Just before the opening of the 1947 season, Durocher was suspended from baseball for one year by commissioner Happy Chandler.

Why was Durocher suspended? According to the decision, it was for an accumulation of unpleasant incidents in which he had been involved that the commissioner construed as detrimental to baseball.

But none of these incidents had even been mentioned at a hearing that was held. Durocher, in effect, was suspended without a trial and without even hearing the accusations.

At the height of the Durocher furor, Brooklyn announced they had purchased the contract of Jackie Robinson, thus moving that pioneer to a major league uniform with minimum publicity.

Burt Shotton was then brought out of retirement to manage the Dodgers. Durocher went back to California and faithfully kept quiet all summer.

Durocher came back to manage the Dodgers in 1948 and did so until July of that year. Then came an announcement that I'll never forget: Leo Durocher became the manager of the New York Giants after the resignation of Mel Ott.

The baseball world was stunned. Fans at the Polo Grounds, conditioned for years to hating the Dodgers in general and Durocher in particular, recoiled in horror. But they slowly recovered as the Giants began to move up the league ladder step-by-step. Leo Ernest Durocher would become the little shepherd at Coogan's Bluff.*

Another phenomenal manager was Frank Robinson. He joined the Cincinnati Reds in 1956 as an outfielder and became the National League's Rookie of the Year. His 38 home runs tied him with Wally Berger of the 1930 Braves (most home runs by a player in his rookie season).

I had my sports show at WWRL, and I had to get him on my broadcast. He reluctantly came on the show at Small's Paradise, a

---

*The Polo Grounds were situated in a hollow overlooked by a minicliff known as Coogan's Bluff.

famous Harlem night spot. Even in his fledgling campaign year, Frank was difficult. He had an attitude—often recalcitrant, irritable. Once he got on the show, things moved along very well.

He was named Most Valuable Player in 1961.

On December 9, 1965, Cincinnati traded him to the Baltimore Orioles. Frank was furious about it because Bill De Witt thought he was "old," at thirty. What is age? (Recently Tom Seaver, the powerhouse of the New York Mets, also *may* have been thought of in the same way. The powerful White Sox picked up his contract, and within the same framework, Seaver may destroy the Mets.)

But, anyway, Frank Robinson in his first year, 1966, with the Orioles led the American League in batting, home runs, and runs batted in. I like that kind of old man. The following year he became the eighth player to reach the $100,000 salary mark.

Robinson stayed with the Orioles, followed by brief stints with Los Angeles, California, and the Cleveland Indians. Despite his extraordinary career, the most sensational part is that on October 3, 1974, Frank Robinson, thirty-nine years young, was hired by the Cleveland Indians as major league's first Black manager. And he thought it couldn't and wouldn't be done.

A lot of adulation was showered on Frank from President Gerald Ford all the way to the guy next door. One thing about Frank, he gave credit where credit was due.

When he brought his Cleveland Indians to Yankee Stadium in 1975, we talked again. I told him how proud I was of his appointment as the first Black major league manager. In his usual poised and unsmiling manner, he said, "Jackie was much more important than what I am doing." It will be a happy day when people do not have to be designated "the first Black player; the first Black manager"; as well as "the first Black Miss America." The definition possibly should be "Miss America who happens to be Black will reign this year"; "Frank Robinson who manages the San Francisco Giants is an American of Black heritage," etc., etc., etc.

Yet we must deal with the reality of America. Twenty years earlier Jackie's breakthrough made for Frank's.

In 1984 Lawrence Peter Berra—better known as Yogi—was named the New York Yankee manager for the second time. A fine selection indeed. Yogi is an astute baseball guy who has the ability, warmth, and sensitivity to lead any good ball club to its pinnacle.

Yogi grew up in a ghetto in St. Louis called the Hill. Although rejected by both the Browns and the Cardinals, he impressed Leo Browne, head of the American League baseball program, and found his way into the Yankee organization.

Yogi played successfully for eighteen years. He was an outstanding backstopper, and even with his awkward build he had the grace and reflexes of a thoroughbred cat, and boy could he hit that rock.

Yogi managed the Yankees to a pennant in 1964 and later the New York Mets in 1973. He was elected to the Baseball Hall of Fame in 1972.

Berra has gained the reputation of being a clown and a clod. When asked about Bill Dickey's tutoring, Yogi replied, "Dickey is learning me all his experience." In 1947 the people of St. Louis held a Yogi Berra Night before a Brown/Yankee game. Yogi told the crowd, "I want to thank everyone for making this night necessary."

That's funny, but that does not make one a "funny-type" person. There are special people tinged with a marvelous madness. We very ordinary people need them to nudge us, to force us to a state of performance for the better good of all people.

Genius is a rare commodity, but it can be found everywhere. Who can deny the spectacular grace of a Joe DiMaggio, the power of a Joe Louis, and the charisma of a Muhammad Ali? There are many forms of genius. Building a better bomb makes you a genius? I'd rather have the genius of a good car mechanic.

And where does Yogi fit in this pattern? Right up there, my friend. He is a clown, we laugh, but he carries a lot of strength.

Yogi Berra has a specificity that lends a kind of unique responsiveness to a unique American game called baseball. He makes it good.

I can see Yogi now, sitting in his underwear in front of his locker at Shea Stadium after the Mets had beaten the Baltimore Orioles in the 1969 World Series.

Yogi was holding a bottle of Yoo-Hoo and looked up at me and said, "Art, I can't believe it." Whenever possible Yogi and I both love talking about and bringing back memories of his St. Louis Browns and the Cardinals. He really hems me in. He too is in the Hall of Fame.

And then there came a thunderbolt, a monsoon from Berkeley, California. They call him Billy the Kid or the Brat, but his rightful name is Alfred Manuel Martin. In his yo-yo contest with the club he was manager of the New York Yankees until replaced by Yogi Berra in the fall of 1983.

Billy is a tough disciplinarian and I think tactically the closest thing to Leo Durocher I ever saw. I like and respect Billy. He's a very sensitive man, but by the same token, he won't take any shit.

In the late forties Billy was with the Oakland Oaks of the Pacific Coast League under manager Casey Stengel. Casey induced the owners to obtain Billy, who began his major league career under Casey in 1950 after a most impressive spring training. One thing I'll give Casey: The old codger could see talent.

Always a scrapper and an aggressive man, Martin opposed injustice. In the early days it was a philosophy of "Hit me and I'll hit you harder," a kind of "eye for an eye" dictate.

Billy started out as a utility infielder in 1950 and 1951, and then became the regular Yankee second baseman in 1952 and 1953; in 1954 military service intervened and he returned to the club the following year. He was a good contact hitter and seemed to thrive in pressure situations.

Billy's World Series play was scintillating. He is tied for fourth on the All-Time Series list for 3 base hits. His lifetime Series batting average of .333 places him in fourteenth place on the All-Time Series records.

My late friend Georgie and I saw Billy hit a 3-run homer in game two of the 1952 Series to lead the Yankees to a 7–1 win over the Dodgers. Then we saw Billy save the 1952 Series for the Yankees in the seventh game with a clutch grab par excellence—a straining catch of a fierce windblown infield popup by Jackie Robinson late in the contest with two outs and the bases loaded with Dodgers.

On May 16, 1957, Billy's so-called scandal erupted at the

Copacabana Club in New York. Billy and five other teammates with their wives (and a girlfriend) were out for a good time. Sammy Davis, Jr., was performing. To complete the scenario, a group of drunken bowlers were also celebrating. The bowlers were loudly uttering racial epithets about Sammy Davis. The Yankees just as loudly protested the derogatory remarks as well as the interruption of the show. At this point the bouncers of the club became involved, and fists were flying—whose we will never know. One of the bowlers was hurt.

It hit the papers in a spectacular manner. But the newspapers printed only part of the story. (Don't believe everything you read.) They left out the Sammy Davis thing and racism. I knew about it because I was a sportscaster at WWRL.

Well, this is just what Yankee general manager George Weiss wanted to hear. Weiss blamed Billy for the entire incident. Weiss disliked Martin and used the Copacabana incident as a reason to trade him to the Kansas City Athletics.

Going from Detroit to Cleveland, Cincinnati, Milwaukee, and Minnesota, he was a traveling man. From 1957 to 1961 he was dealt umpteen times. Why? Billy was a difficult man. He refused to take any guff from anyone.

After managerial stints with Minnesota, Detroit, and Texas, Billy returned to the Yankees as a manager in 1975. His ball clubs won the 1976 American League Flag and 1977 World Championship. Billy "resigned" as Yankee helmsman during the summer of 1978, but returned to the mentorship in a startling announcement on Old Timers' Day in 1979. Unfortunately, he was dismissed again from the Yankees by George Steinbrenner in October of the same year. He then joined the Oakland As, leading them to a surprising second-place finish in 1980.

Billy remained with the As until 1983, when he rejoined the Yankees, only to be replaced by Yogi Berra in the fall of the year.

I had the opportunity to speak with Jeff Burroughs, who under Billy's tutelage won the Most Valuable Player Award in 1974 when Martin managed him with the Texas Rangers.

Burroughs told me that Martin isn't like some managers who think they are your father; Billy treats you like a man. He said that Billy really knows how to teach you to win and that's all he is

91

interested in. He knew that Martin really didn't care about the superstars—all he wanted was for the ball club to work as a unit for the sole purpose of winning. Burroughs knew that Billy would protect you from all sides so that you could concentrate on your work.

Another admirer, Frank Quilice, onetime manager of the Minnesota Twins, told me that Billy is one of the best ever. He said that Billy was a smart baseball guy. His quick temper on the field, Quilice feels, has to do with what Billy feels is an injustice and unnecessary interference from others.

In 1983 I seriously began observing Billy. From the diamond to the dugout to the clubhouse to the press box, something was happening to Billy. The fire, the intensity, the total concentration on the game seemed to dwindle. He seemed preoccupied with his health.

It was during this period that he slowly, quietly lost the confidence of his ball club. Each Yankee seemed to be going his own way, and so was Billy.

When he was replaced by Yogi, he received a "front office" job.

Come back soon, Billy Boy, Billy Boy.

There is a daring that I have admired in all my heroes. They are like downhill racers. What powers enter the body, mind, and emotional psyche that would possess any rational human being to ski downhill on ice? But to be human is a monstrous responsibility, and we took the option to stop sleeping in trees and randomly eating berries like the gorilla, the orangutan, and the chimpanzee. We were willing to take the risk.

My boyhood idol was John Joseph McGraw. I didn't know the man and I never saw him, but my father painted so vivid a picture of a man of courage and daring, a man so irascible and yet who could be so charming, a baseball manager par excellence.

John McGraw, born in Truxton, New York, on April 7, 1873, had a difficult childhood. (His mother, three brothers, and a stepsister died of diphtheria.) Perhaps he felt deserted and decided to turn around and give it back to the world. At any rate this little Napoleon, weighing in at 120 pounds, had a passion for baseball

and the talent of a giant. In the 1890s he was playing third base
with the old "blood and guts" Baltimore Orioles. He was outrageous, threw a baseball at umpire Bob Emslie, punched out umpire Bill Bryon for saying he had been "run out" of Baltimore,
and had the supreme audacity to curse out National League president John Tener for fining and suspending him.

I read everything about him because, contrary to opinion, I was
not there in the 1890s. Red Barber, Grantland Rice talked and
wrote about him. He was my kind of guy. McGraw wouldn't take
any kind of guff from anyone.

Then he was appointed manager of the last-place New York Giants in 1902.

He ranted, raved, and bullied that second-rate major league club
to win five pennants and by a hair's breadth missed one more pennant in his first twelve years. The next dozen years he clawed his
way to five more.

McGraw was an arrogant tyrant king, but most of his players
loved him—and those who did not at least admired him.

For thirty years he managed the Giants, and they finally won the
success that McGraw knew was rightfully theirs. In his fashion, he
accorded them the development of their natural talents. McGraw
invented inside baseball—bunt, hit, and run and steal. With his
extraordinary strategy he evolved the freer use of the Platoon system as well as the specialized development of players according to
their peculiar and particular strengths.

There was something about McGraw and the aura he exuded—
the pushing, innovative mover that thrust this sometimes pedantic
precise chess game into an emotional frenzy as no manager had
ever done before. He incited fans into a cheering mob either for or
against the Giants. Who knows how many fanatical observers of
the game he incited, who in their very enthusiasm encouraged others to join in this great contest?

Grantland Rice, famed sportswriter of the time, noted that
McGraw's stance, his challenging walk across the field, brought
cheers and jeers from the crowd. But the crowds multiplied just as
at a Joe Louis fight, a Muhammad Ali contest. I think that is what
charisma is all about.

McGraw had a lot of nerve. In 1901 and 1902 when he was

managing the Baltimore Orioles in the new American League, McGraw knew he needed new, fresh, strong ballplayers. And much to the disdain of Charles Comiskey, president of the Chicago White Sox, McGraw had the unmitigated gall to try to slip in some Black players.

My older friend Mr. Grant of St. Nicholas Avenue told me this story: When the Orioles were in training in Hot Springs, Arkansas, they were based at the Eastland Hotel. All of the help was Black.

Black ballplayers had little choice about the nature of their work at that time. One of the bellboys at the Eastland Hotel was Charles Grant, a Black guy. Grant had been second baseman for the Columbia Giants, a Chicago Black team, the year before.

Well, anyway, Grant and several other employees at the hotel idled away their free time playing baseball on the grounds. Naturally, McGraw watched and saw that Grant had major league ability. Now let's put McGraw in his proper perspective. He had not the slightest concern about the "Black man's plight." McGraw was an honest man. If you could do the job, then you had the job. McGraw's problem was how could he pass off a Black man in a "white man's game" in the perilous times of 1901. He had to think of a ruse. McGraw had no reservations about the ability of Charles Grant, but in these especially overtly racial times McGraw came up with an answer.

Every white American knew how badly the Indian had been treated in the procurement of his land, and McGraw probably depended upon the guilt factor. So, clever man that he was, McGraw decided to pass Grant off as an American Indian playing second base.

This was an interesting concept because it implied that if you were not a known American Black, you could be anything.

I still remember stories about some American Blacks who decided to play games with the white national racial concept of what comprised a Negro. A Negro was nothing but a nigger. So consistent with this concept was the "nigger" who defied it. Those Blacks walked all over Georgia, Alabama, Mississippi wearing turbans and speaking gibberish, so that they were considered foreign and were accepted but with trepidation.

So McGraw decided to pass off Charles Grant as an Indian.

With war paint and feathers stuck in his kinky hair, Charles Grant—now Cherokee Indian—could be the crack second baseman for the team. Unfortunately, after a short spell (Grant never appeared in a regular season major league game), president of the Chicago White Sox, Charles Comiskey, ferreted out the fact that the Cherokee Indian was really Grant, the son of a Negro horse trainer from Cincinnati, and Grant was consequently fired. Too bad for baseball; too bad for America; there was a long furrow to plow.

But McGraw was still looking for good baseball players. His interest drove him into the rich deposits in the Caribbean. There was a fireballing Cuban Black pitcher, Jose Mendez, who, at the height of his artistry on the mound and at the growing power of McGraw, was seriously considered. And then there was Andrew (Rube) Foster, just a plain Black American, who was at the height of his career—another consideration.

As tough as McGraw was, he had walked through sacred waters and decided not to defy again the sensibilities of organized baseball leaders by signing a man of color. Pity!

I suppose, in a way of compensation, he hired the Black Eddie MacKall as a "rubber." He brought him from Baltimore to join the Giants. A rubber is a massager, but MacKall was really a trainer, and by the evidence given, the Giants continued to progress.

I felt sorry when I read about MacKall. He had to be designated as a rubber when he was really a trainer. I'm with James Baldwin when he says, "Call me by my rightful name."

John McGraw, you were one hell of a man.

William Harrison Southworth was another manager I loved as a kid. The contrast between Southworth and McGraw was quite definitive. The latter gruff, tough, and unyielding; the former gentle, quiet, and understanding. Yet both succeeded as top managers. Despite the gruffness of one and in spite of the laid back attitude of the other, there was a similar quality in both men—talent. One masked his sensitivity, the other displayed it, yet it was recognized by the ballplayers and they responded to it. I think it just proves that there's a place for everyone in this world if you just look.

Billy Southworth was one of seven children born to blacksmith Orlando Southworth on March 9, 1893, in Harvard, Nebraska. The family moved to Columbus, Ohio, when Billy was nine. Billy was immediately attracted to baseball, much to the disdain of his parents, and he persevered.

When Southworth was only twenty he delivered a game-winning triple for Toledo in 1913, but the incident taught him a lesson. Jim Sheckard, Toledo's manager, had given Billy the bunt sign. When queried, Billy responded flippantly, "What's the difference. I won the game anyway." Sheckard responded, "The bunt sign was on, and you're benched."

It reminds me of stories my wife told me when she was teaching school. She'd ask a student a question, and they'd come up with all sorts of interesting tidbits, curlicues, and whatevers. She would just look them straight in the eye and say, "Answer the question asked, or I'll fail you." The logistics of this is of course discipline.

In 1928 Sam Breadon, owner of the St. Louis Cardinals, was feeling down low. He could understand his team being defeated, but having the hell beat out of them four straight games by the New York Yankees in the World Series appalled him. He demoted Bill McKechnie to the class AA farm in Rochester, and brought Billy Southworth, by now playing manager of the Rochester Red Wings, in 1929 to St. Louis for Billy the Kid's first fling at the Cardinals' managerial position.

Billy Southworth had been one of the boys when he was a playing member of the Cardinals. He sang with them and occasionally had a prohibition-forbidden highball with the boys. In short, he had been the nice guy. But, in a mosaic major league career, he had been under some tough managers—Joe Birmingham in Cleveland, George Stallings in Boston, John McGraw in New York, and Rogers Hornsby in St. Louis. Southworth, a fellow with a naturally sweet disposition, felt he had to emulate these men—to be tough with his former fellow players to command their respect. In later years he admitted it was his big mistake in his first major league managerial venture.

The Cardinals trained in Avon Park, Florida, in 1929. Most of the players had been in two rich World Series in 1926 and 1928;

they were signed for good salaries—and were in the money. A number had not only their wives at the camp but their cars. The Cardinals had an exhibition game scheduled in Miami, and Billy heard some of his players were contemplating driving there.

He held a meeting in his clubhouse and said, "We go to Miami tomorrow, and we go by train. There won't be any riding in automobiles to Miami with your family and friends. I hope everybody gets that."

As the meeting broke up, someone said, "Heel" under his breath but loud enough for all to hear. Later Southworth, believing that two players were having a party in their room, entered the chamber, only to find both men in bed. It didn't make him any more popular with the squad.

By July the Cardinals were so fouled up with anti-Southworth sentiment that he was demoted back to Rochester.

But like the Phoenix he arose. His Rochester Red Wing team won a pennant that year and again in 1930 and 1931. Then he was supposedly rewarded when they moved him to Columbus in 1932—the club finished last. His wife died and again a previous drinking problem erupted and he was dropped from the St. Louis chair.

Then in 1933 New York Giants manager Bill Terry took Southworth on, but he left the club in spring training. I'm not saying anything of a serious nature occurred, but the day after Southworth left, Terry had a black eye—draw your own conclusions.

Obviously angry and disillusioned, Southworth went into the cottonseed oil business and remarried. He stopped drinking and stayed away from baseball for two years. But that particular man Branch Rickey with his special intuitive nose for talent ferreted out Southworth in 1935 in the belief that he deserved another chance. Cautious Rickey offered him a chance at the bottom rung of the Cardinal ladder, for $300 a month. Billy accepted the job of managing the Asheville, North Carolina team. Then began Billy Southworth's comeback.

Rickey had the sensitivity not to dictate to Southworth how to do his job and gave him his full head. It worked like a charm. There are people in this world who do not need instruction in how to do their job, and Rickey had the insight to divine this. Southworth won the pennant that year.

From there he moved to Memphis in 1936. Continuing on his streak, the Southern Association club earned $100,000 from the sale of players developed by Southworth. In 1939 it was back to Rochester. Still climbing, Southworth proved the adage—if at first you don't succeed, try, try, try, try again.

In the 1940 season when manager Ray Blades was fired, Rickey called for Southworth. At this point it was obvious that Southworth was a different man from the man they had had in 1929. Far more mature, more decisive, and even more clever. Some of us are late bloomers.

The 1940 club was staggering along in the second division when Southworth went to the helm. And his magic lifted the ball club to a third place finish. Then in 1941, despite the fact that President Breadon sold some $300,000 worth of ballplayers, Southworth's crew managed a second-place finish.

In 1942 Billy broke St. Louis's eight-year championship deprivation with the first of three consecutive National League pennants.

It was at this point I became totally aware of the magnetism of the man and his special kind of genius. I loved Billy Southworth. I can see this handsome-visaged man in the visiting team's dugout at the Polo Grounds with one foot on the lip of that enclave. Still, sadly I remember the many times during World War II seeing Southworth's son at the Polo Grounds. He was an Air Force pilot, and he sat in the box seats behind the visiting team's dugout. Sometimes certain people seemed marked for tragedy despite their talents and sincerity. Billy, Jr., died when his B29 crashed into Flushing Bay. Southworth never got over that, and neither would I if placed in a similar position.

I had the singular pleasure of meeting Southworth in 1942 when I was somewhere between fourteen and fifteen years of age. He signed a photograph for me and was quite gracious about it. I had photos of all the St. Louis Cardinals, which I purchased via mail from Burke and Brace photographs out of Chicago.

The 1942 St. Louis Cardinals' winning the National League pennant and the World Series just has to be my number one baseball thrill. This was togetherness at its best: Stan Musial in his first full year, Terry Moore, Enos Slaughter, Whitey Kurowski, Mort Cooper, Walker Cooper, Johnny Beazley, and a pack of other Cardinals pulling as one, under the deft guidance of Southworth.

He could have had Buck Newsom that year, but said Southworth, the peripatetic pitcher "isn't our type." Billy wanted players with a common purpose.

Even when the Cardinals were under the staggering impost of a 10-game deficit as late as August 9, behind the Brooklyn Dodgers, Billy kept driving St. Louis. And oh, how he drove them. The Cardinals wound up winning 43 of their last 52 games and soared to their first pennant since 1934.

St. Louis went on to wipe out the Yankees in 5 games in the World Series.

As Branch Rickey said in 1942, "Southworth is the perfect manager . . . gentlemanly, shrewd, and inspirational."

Billy Southworth was the friend of every man on his ball club, and they knew it. They came to him with personal problems as well as those concerning baseball. Even if a man had made a stupid blunder, Southworth didn't bawl out the player until the next day. Then both he and the athlete would have had a night's sleep on it. He was a strict disciplinarian but not in the sense of a John McGraw. Southworth was known as baseball's Little Gentleman, but he carried an iron fist in his velvet glove.

You can't write a book about baseball managers without including one of the greatest strategists, Joseph Vincent McCarthy. He did not have the personality flair of a McGraw, but he had his own special kind of genius.

McCarthy was born April 21, 1887, in Germantown, Pennsylvania. Joe's father died when he was three and life was poor and tough and that shapes character.

In finance Joe was never an extravagant man, and that early need for frugality carried over into his personal life as well as baseball. It served him well and baseball also.

Joe's demeanor might have appeared cold, and he was as calculating as a computer, but he knew everything that was happening on or off the field. His eye was a wide-range camera. While observing the batter, Joe's peripheral vision also knew exactly where the left fielder was playing.

He had the gift of immediately recognizing potentiality and forced it to its ultimate goal. Under McCarthy's tutelage, Red Rolfe became one of the greatest third basemen in the American League, although he had come to the Yankees as a shortstop. Another shortstop, Joe Gordon, became one of the best second baseman imaginable. McCarthy even stunned these young men who didn't know what happened to them—but suddenly they were stars.

Before he entered the Yankee organization, McCarthy was brought from Louisville of the American Association in 1926 to take charge of the Chicago Cubs by owner William Wrigley. With McCarthy's great organizational skill, he soon had the club in order.

With McCarthy riding herd, the Cubs came from eighth place in 1925 to fourth in 1926, fourth in 1927, and third in 1928. Joe won his first major league pennant in 1929. It was the first time the Cubs were able to win a flag since 1918, that war-depleted season.

In the 1929 World Series the Cubs caught hell from Connie Mack's Philadelphia Athletics.

The Cubs were the receivers of the humiliation of the much-discussed 10-run eighth inning in the fourth game at Shibe Park on October 12. They were leading 8–0, and it seemed that they would draw the Series even with the Athletics at 2 games apiece.

My friend Joe Grant was there and enchanted me with a phenomenon that has never been repeated as of this writing. Grant said the 10-run inning, the biggest in World Series competition, all began when Cub outfielder Hack Wilson misjudged a Mule Haas drive that fell behind him for an inside-the-park home run.

It was also Grant's belief that the sun got into Wilson's eye.

Mr. Grant told me that was the coming demise of McCarthy in the Windy City and he resigned before the 1930 season.

Ed Barrow, general manager of the New York Yankees, had heard via a popular sportswriter and a friend of McCarthy's that McCarthy would soon be availble. Thank God for good friends! Barrow, of course, had easily recognized the extraordinary talent

McCarthy had and that the World Series incident was merely an unfortunate fluke.

Barrow relayed the information and his intuitive feelings to Colonel Ruppert, then owner of the Yankees. Well Colonel Ruppert knew how to delegate authority and followed Barrow's advice.

Thereafter, McCarthy became manager and served a long tenure as Yankee manager, 1931–1946. Although McCarthy was titled Second-Place Joe, the Yankees won the 1932 pennant and world championship in his second year. For three consecutive years the Yankees finished second, but that was a major improvement.

Ah, but then the tide turned. With Joe DiMaggio joining the already present Lou Gehrig, the Yankees won four straight pennants—and world championships 1936 through 1939. McCarthy's club finished in third place in 1940. Then they came back to win a pennant and a World Series in 1941. Another flag in 1942, and a pennant and world title in 1943.

You know the cheese stands alone, and Joe McCarthy's record does too. World War II blemished his career in that his key stars were called into the military. In 1944 the Yankees finished third, and in 1945 they finished fourth.

In 1945 the new Yankee owners, Larry MacPhail, Dan Topping, and Del Webb did not share the same type of camaraderie McCarthy had enjoyed with Ruppert and Barrow. McCarthy's health declined, and he suffered a mild breakdown in 1946.

There comes a time when the pressures pursue too persistently. McCarthy never lost faith in himself but was disappointed when he felt others had. McCarthy "gave up," retired, and became a farmer.

But "How're you gonna keep them down on the farm after they've seen Paris?" In 1948 Joe joined the Boston Red Sox, whom he managed for three seasons. Joe lost a one-game playoff to the Cleveland Indians in 1948, and the Yankees beat him in 1949 on the last two days of the season, thus excluding him from obtaining the pennant.

Despite this, Joseph McCarthy was immortalized by the famed sportswriter Grantland Rice. The latter felt that McCarthy, John McGraw, and Connie Mack were the best managers that existed up to that point in time.

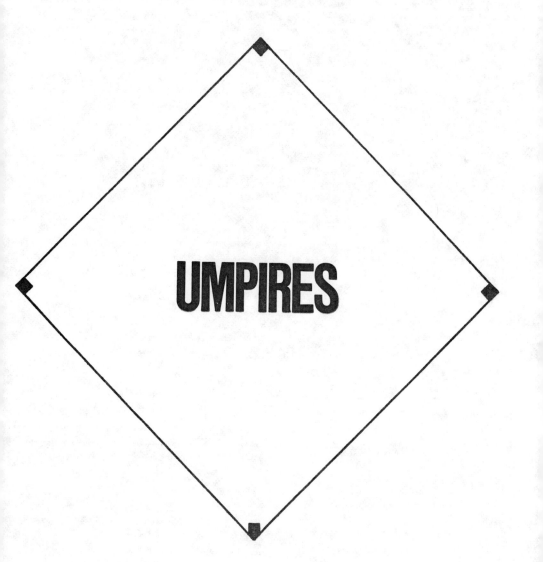

UMPIRES

When I was a kid, I loved everything about baseball. The umpires to me were King Solomons. I was fascinated by them. I envied them. I never considered that that was a job because at my youthful age I would have done it for nothing. According to my thinking then and on questionable level now, the umpire is the judge as well as the prosecuting attorney and as a consequence was naturally harassed and ofttimes admired and hated. Now that I am much older, wanting to be an umpire is tantamount to wanting to be President of the United States. I can admire their fierce sense of responsibility, whether they are right or wrong, but sometimes it comes down to being a thankless job; however, the job must be done.

There are five umpires in the Baseball Hall of Fame: National Leaguers Bill Klem, "Jocko" Conlan; in the American League we have Billy Evans, Cal Hubbard, and Tommy Connolly.

Klem started his thirty-five-year career in 1905. Klem had style. He was majestic, regal; he used exaggerated gesticulations to make his calls. Klem actually originated arm signals to call balls and strikes. In his first sixteen major league seasons Klem worked exclusively behind home plate—because of his excellence and accuracy in calling balls and strikes—even after the two-umpire system came into being shortly after World War II. He won a record number of World Series assignments, eighteen in all, because of his particular skills. He was in charge at all times. He states, "Baseball is more than a game to me—it's a religion." I echo his thoughts, because it is the same way with me.

Klem was a tough cookie. John M. McGraw, the powerful martinet from Truxton, New York, became incensed with some of Klem's calls and threatened to strip Klem of his job. I love Klem; he replied, "Mister Manager, if it's possible for you to take my job away from me, I don't want it." Don't you love that kind of security of self?

Klem had an unusual way of dealing with fuming managers and raging players. He would simply drag his spikes in the dirt, making the line. If a manager or player crossed it, he was automatically banished from the game. No one ever took up the challenge.

Klem did more than any other umpire to improve working conditions for his lodge members. Getting proper dressing facilities for the umpires was his first step. A startled National League commissioner, Harry Pulliam, wanted to know why umpires needed their own changing rooms.

"It's embarrassing to be on a streetcar in uniform after the game, especially when the home team has lost," retorted an incensed Klem.

Not only was it embarrassing, it was also dangerous.

Shortly before Klem died, he described a 1941 game in which he stated, "I walked away from the beefing ballplayer saying to myself, 'I'm almost certain Billy Herman tagged him.' Then it came to me, and I almost wept. For the first time in my career I only thought a man was tagged." Klem retired after that afternoon. But only a giant can recognize his failing powers, and I have the greatest respect in the world for the man.

Then there was Tom Connolly and, would you believe, an Englishman. Connolly started his career as an umpire in 1898 with the National League; however, Connie Mack, manager of the Philadelphia Athletics, was so impressed by the man he recommended him to the American League in 1901. Obviously Ban Johnson believed Connie Mack, and Tom Connolly umpired in the majors for thirty-four seasons. I never saw Connolly personally, but my friend Joe Grant told me that though he did not have the same flair as Klem, you nonetheless were impressed by his no nonsense posture. Connolly reminded me of an elementary school teacher I had, Anita Cherry. She was strict on discipline, but there was a special kindness and compassion that she tried to keep hidden. Tom Connolly reminded me of her. A strict disciplinarian, but for a period of ten years he never threw a player out of a game. Softhearted sucker and my kind of guy.

Another one of my kind of guys was Billy Evans. I love the look of a fastidious man. Billy Evans was neat at all times. His visual as well as verbal fastidiousness made him outstanding in his field. The game of baseball was a real blood-and-guts kind of competition. Amenities were seldom par for the course, yet Billy Evans radiated a special kind of refinement that probably helped make the game more civilized. At the bare age of twenty-two, he came in as a major league umpire in 1906. Evans's career continued through 1927. It certainly was merited that he went on to become a front office executive. He had that special savoir faire to make human beings act like human beings.

Then there was Cal Hubbard. Cal was such a big imposing-looking man that you knew instinctively that you'd never lean on him. As sassy as I was as a kid, if Cal were umpiring our stickball and sandlot games, I would have revered his opinions. Hubbard was 6'3" and 250 pounds—formidable. His very appearance gave him the authoritative posture that immediately gained respect. But that is not all of it; it was really all about his keen intelligence. In 1936 he arrived in the American League system after an eight-year stint in the minors. He retired after fifteen seasons in the major leagues only because of a hunting accident that disabled him. Hubbard has a great share of acclaim; he was the first person to be named to three national sports shrines—baseball, college, and professional football halls of fame.
Wish it were me.

In 1939 I was at the Polo Grounds with my friend Georgie Vaz. It was right after the all-star game break in early July. The New

York Giants were playing the third game of a three-contest set-to with the Cincinnati Reds. Giants' Harry Gumbert held a 4–3 lead over Gene Thompson as the Reds came to bat in the eighth inning. With a runner on, Cincinnati's Harry Craft lined a low curving drive into the lower left field stands at the foul pole. Plate umpire Lee Ballanfant ruled it a fair ball, thus pulling the Reds into a 5–4 lead. Harry Danning, Giant catcher, stormed around Ballanfant, proceeded to shove the official, and shouted his protest of the call.

When you deal with emotions, you have to be a pretty cool character or deal back in kind. Ballanfant tried to be cool, but his patience was at last exhausted, and Danning was thumbed out of the game.

This was only the beginning; the protest was building. The Giants took their case to Ziggy Sears, who was umpiring at second. After a long harangue with Sears, Giant left fielder Jo-Jo Moore, who claimed he had the best view of the ball when it passed the foul pole, was thrown out of the game.

The Giants animatedly continued their verbal assault, and when big George Magerkurth, the first base umpire, decided to move up to home plate to deal with the matter, he encountered Giant short-stop Billy Jurges and they had a brief "discussion."

Later, and according to Magerkurth's rendition, Jurges shouted at him, "Don't you spit in my face." Magerkurth with quiet fury and reddening face replied, "Don't get your face so near mine, and it won't get spit on." Jurges freaked out and responded, "I'll spit on yours." By this time the macho image, the image that diplomacy should never know, zoomed forth. Magerkurth bellowed, "I'd like to see you do that." Jurges obliged him. Come on, who likes someone to spit on you? Magerkurth belted Jurges in the ribs, and Jurges responded with a punch to the umpire's jaw.

Of course I couldn't hear what was going on, but I saw the aftermath of the repercussion. It was a kind of chaos I'll never forget. No one should let himself get out of control that much unless it is for a more important reason.

Anyway, the next day the National League president announced an immediate ten-day suspension for both Jurges and Magerkurth, and each was fined $150.

The incident may seem like child's play, but to a baseball historian it is highly significant. As a result of that to-do, the installation of a net along the length of each Polo Grounds foul pole aided umpires in determining whether balls hit to the poles were fair or foul. Many of today's ballparks are similarly equipped.

What is always interesting about these events in baseball history is, of course, the extraordinary people involved. Leo Durocher is quoted as saying Magerkurth "always chewed tobacco, and when he got mad he'd get to spluttering and stuttering." A very dangerous combination when you're engaged in any kind of nose-to-nose confrontation.

Well, I think Magerkurth met his match in Jurges.

Joe Grant used to tell me about Ty Cobb winning unanimous decisions over umpire Billy Evans under the grandstands.

My friend Georgie Vaz and I saw a fan attack umpire George Moriarty after a game in Ebbets Field in 1939. This is the same Moriarty who my father tells me battled several Chicago White Sox at Cleveland after a doubleheader defeat on Memorial Day 1932. Pitcher Milt Gaston, who started the melee beneath the stands, and Chicago manager Lew Fonseca were fined $500 each, catcher Charlie Berry (later an umpire) $250, and catcher Frank Grube $100.

There comes a time when you grow up when you don't know which came first—the chicken or the egg. Do laws change behavior, or does behavior change laws, and possibly conditions? I tend to think toward the latter, but I may be wrong. I was always in love with baseball, and while my parents were too, they did not foresee any kind of future in it for their Black child.

I tried to follow their dictates, but after a year at law school, I just said the hell with it. I married the lady from Hunter College whom I was in love with and decided to take the dare. I applied for a job at radio station WWRL in Woodside, New York. Just like some people want to be in movies, my thrust was that I wanted to be on radio. I was hired to do merchandising, which is a fancy way of saying "Hang up advertising posters all over the city." It was 1955, and there was a recession; to me it was a depression. I had a brand-new wife, a cute little apartment. I had to take anything to sustain us, but I was getting closer to my goal—WWRL was a community station. Community station generally meant all Black, just like the new term urban redevelopment. However, I managed to enchant Fred Barr, program director of the station, and in a couple of months I had a Sunday night sports show. There was an excellent response to me after my early fluffing. Soon thereafter I did not have to hang posters all over the city and had a regular daily spot on the radio. I thought I was Red Barber, Ted Husing, all the greats mixed together, and became relatively complacent.

I felt this was my niche, and I felt that I was lucky to get it. Yet there were many machinations taking place or natural explosions about to erupt. Chief Justice Earl Warren announced in May 1954 the Supreme Court's unanimous decision that declared, "We conclude that in the field of public education the doctrine of 'separate but equal' has no place. Separate facilities are inherently unequal." Now here was a crack in the door.

I think that most Blacks considered this a long sought after kind of redemption and they wanted to see what might occur. There was the Little Rock, Arkansas, debacle, and there was Dr. Martin Luther King, Jr., preaching a philosophy of nonviolence and at the same time "creative disorder"—protest marches and demonstrations. Dr. King accomplished many important things. His use of nonviolence was certainly a magnificent ploy, because it required the true use of law and order by federal intervention when the local authorities would not intervene in the violence that the white population was perpetrating.

The Black population tried, but by August 11, 1965, in an area of Los Angeles called Watts, the explosion began. There were no jobs. The young were so frustrated by their inabilities to secure employment and support their families they went on a rampage. The excuse, not the reason, for the riot revolved around what was considered police action and their manhandling a Black arrested man. In their fury the Blacks destroyed what little they had because it didn't seem to make any difference anyway. They ran through the streets shouting, "Burn, baby, burn."

There is something contagious about violence, and the pent-up frustrations that wrecked Watts spread to places all over the United States.

I vaguely remember the Harlem riot in the early thirties that constituted one of the major riots there. A young kid went into a five-and-ten on 125th Street; someone thought he was stealing something. (I don't know; perhaps he was; it was a period of bad times.) The situation on 125th Street was overripe. Although this was an area where mostly Black people lived, it was chiefly white people who owned the businesses and made the money from them. The banks, ha, ha, ha, gave you no money to institute your own business in your segregated area; the whites who owned the apartment buildings charged you more rent than you would have had to pay for equivalent housing elsewhere in the city; and the white food-store owners charged you more for your secondhand food. In addition, the schools appeared just not to give a damn.

So when the police were called and this very young Black boy was taken to the basement area of the five-and-ten to be questioned and by chance shortly afterward a funeral van drew up to the rear of the five-and-ten, the silent crowd became hostile. The rumors of a child murdered by the police—the authority figures—rang out loudly. Fortunately none of this was true, but the incident ignited a deep-seated resentment that was monumental. Even on Sugar Hill we felt the repercussions. There was destruction everywhere—destroy what you are not permitted to conquer.

After the riot my future mother-in-law Edna Hayes worked on the mayor's Committee on Conditions in Harlem. After two years of study and research, they came up with the conclusion that the Harlem riot occurred because of discrimination. No kidding!

So when Watts rioted, I already understood. Then there was Detroit and Newark. Millions and millions of dollars worth of damage and many, many deaths. Something had to be done.

I truly believe that when the Blacks finally said enough, and because they were being destructive about it, changes occurred.

In my particular case, I was finally contacted by NBC radio to interview for a sports show. Fine! I know what I'm doing and what I'm about. I got the job and was able to leave WWRL for a comparatively decent salary. But what a shame that a relatively middle-class Black got the plum that so many poor underprivileged Blacks had fought, died, and gone to prison for.

From radio I almost immediately went into TV as a regular reporter. It was fascinating but not really my forte. I wanted the sports—here I knew I was supreme. Finally I was occasionally filling in for Kyle Rote, the sports guy, and anchoring on the weekends. (TV stations did that with Blacks, and some still do.) Weekend anchorman and most times odd hours. Maybe they thought Blacks were not ready for prime time. Or they were not prepared to view us on a regular basis.

Nonetheless, I gained a certain acclaim back in the dark days of the sixties. But I had immediate accessibility to dugouts and club-houses and a good reason to explore and further my knowledge of the upward movement of baseball.

I said all that to say that's how I met Emmett L. Ashford, the first Black umpire in major league baseball, as well as countless other special athletes, but now I just want to talk about Ashford.

In 1967 Emmett worked the All-Star game in California, and I had the privilege of meeting him. We talked at length, and I learned about what he had encountered. He was born on November 23, 1914, in Los Angeles. Emmett Ashford loved baseball, like any other red-blooded American. He told me that one day in a Los Angeles sandlot game the regular umpire didn't show up. It was 1937. He volunteered his services as an umpire. Hell broke out at a Black's appearance, but he held his guns and surprisingly received a decent sum of money after a collection was taken up around the park.

Although while attending Chapman College in Orange, California, he umpired the college team baseball games, he never considered it as a career. Then World War II came along and interrupted everyone's thoughts of career. When Emmett got out of the Navy in 1947 in Corpus Christi, Texas, he began to have other thoughts. Jackie Robinson had already broken the color barrier, and this stimulated Emmett to seriously think about a career as an umpire.

When Ashford had become involved in umpiring at Chapman College, he had loved the power of it. He began to work as an umpire in the school-system baseball setup. Then he began officiating basketball and football games; after that, USC and UCLA and the entire college circuit. It was at this point that Ashford thought, what the hell—I'll go pro.

UMPIRES

In 1951 the professional scouts who had been following him around when he was umpiring in college arranged a professional appearance for him but not in the United States—in Mexicali, Mexico, where the average temperature is about 115 during the day and 110 at night. He worked a 4-game series on a July Fourth weekend. That experience was a frightening one. Ashford dashed down to Mexicali and told the guard at the border, "Me umpire." Apparently he said the wrong thing because one of the guards picked up a broken beer bottle and said, "You umpire? The last umpire leave here pretty quick." Intimidated but fearless, Ashford went to the ballpark anyway. When he got to the ballpark, the white umpires refused to work with him. The game was held up, and they played Latin music over the P.A. system while they tried to find somebody to work the bases for Ashford.

Finally Emmett was "allowed" to work the entire 4-game series between Mexicali and Tucson behind the plate. Emmett was such a colorful umpire and such a gesticulating performer that the Latins ate him up. He had it made. Ashford was as excited about the Mexicans as they were by him. He rushed to the Postmaster's Office in California where he was working at the time and got a leave of absence to finish off the season in Mexico, and he also worked the play-offs.

You know there is something so extraordinarily exciting about a Black man, or really, I suppose, any man's, being *able* to do the thing he wants to do and do it well.

The following year he received a Mexican contract for the full season of 1952, but he couldn't get a leave of absence from the postal authorities this time. Ashford had fifteen years seniority as a postal employee, but he decided to go for broke. He resigned. Not many people have the courage to give up insured security and a pension plan, and I always admire those who undertake the courage.

Any Black in America has a problem. The problem is simple. Blacks are merely denegrated to the lowest rung. Acknowledgment of said problem poses another problem, and necessarily, Ashford had his misgivings too, and the thought of suicide vaguely crossed his mind. The damn league in Mexico folded. There were six white umpires in the league and fifty-seven minor leagues and there was a problem for them to place him, as a new and a Black umpire. So he headed out to Ensenada, stretched out on the sand, and pondered his life.

Fortunately time, that elemental quandary, saved him. Two days after he was beached, he got a call about a job in El Paso, Texas (Class C). He took it.

When he got to El Paso, unheralded and unsung, he was in for some surprises. There were two policemen there, and by the third inning there were fifteen policemen. The audience response was, at least at that time, usual. One man shouted, "Nigger, why don't you go back to California! I don't want you out there *trying* to do a white man's job."

Emmett told me that he just looked at him over his shoulder and said, "If you go home and put on some shoes, maybe then we can discuss the matter."

His career went that way, with his umpiring the Pacific Coast League, and then finally in 1966 he joined the American League.

Then there is another special person. Somehow this game of baseball prompts or dredges up something intimately important in the development of people. Bernice Gera was one of those people. When a forty-one-year-old Jackson Heights housewife makes her debut as an umpire in the New York–Penn League, I think that's some stuff.

It was in June 1972 in Geneva, New York, and she walked out there to umpire a New York/Pennsylvania doubleheader. After the first game she walked into the office of Joseph McDonough, Geneva's general manager, and said, with tears in her eyes, "I'm sorry, Joe, I just resigned from baseball."

I almost had tears in my eyes when I heard that.

How she even got to be an umpire is a miracle. I had met her, talked with her, and loved the kind of strength she emitted.

But Bernice taught me a lesson. "Life Ain't No Crystal Stair" (according to the great Black poet Langston Hughes's words). I sincerely doubt that anyone on this planet earth would want to experience what Bernice did and still be a winner even if only for one day. The point is to win. Hey, sucker—look out, "I'm coming" was her message.

UMPIRES

I always, I think, understood Bernice, or at least I could be compassionate with her situation. Her story was the story I had heard so many times. I even heard it from the fifteen-minute soap operas that we listened to when we ran home from school to have lunch: "Can a girl from a small mining town in Pennsylvania find happiness in a"—whatever kind of munificent setting that she happened to fall.

Bernice, the youngest of five children, was born in Ernest, Pennsylvania in 1931. According to Bernice, her father was guilty of every vice in the book and her mother ran a close second. Bernice's mother left her, and then when she was two, her father disappeared. She was bandied around from relative to relative throughout her early childhood. But the saving grace was baseball. As the years progressed, little Bernice learned to hit that ball harder, run faster, and curse better than her caretakers—the aunts, uncles, grandmothers, grandfathers who "lended" her their home in a time of strife.

Most of the time she was hungry and had to hit, push, cry, or steal to survive. Bernice was as guilty of that as anyone with intelligence would be confronted with the same circumstances.

At the age of nine she became the town's marble champ. She won the big marble contest, which offered the prizes of a trip to Pittsburgh and a bicycle. Would you believe that she was disqualified because she was a female, and for underwriting they threw in that she was underaged. WOW! No wonder there is a woman's liberation movement. But what took you so long?

Bernice's early life was one of daily physical abuse by her uncles or aunts and the intermittent visits of her vague mother. She lived just the way they tell us niggers lived.

Still there was baseball—the transcendent release, escape, and fulfillment; and she was damned good at it. She hung in there and succeeded, and that's the story of a champion.

When Bernice found the time, when she was an office worker in New York, she gave baseball lessons on weekends and on occasion gave batting demonstrations. She selflessly obliged herself to helping out children in the ghetto areas. She remembered and tried to offer a kind of camaraderie that would make the misery of poverty at least tolerable.

Finally after a long time of going through trials and tribulations of the wrong kind, Bernice Gera, spunky woman, decided "what the hell" and entered an umpiring school in West Palm Beach, Florida. She was the first woman to attend. Upon graduation Bernice took her certificate and went looking for a job. She went straight to the top. The commissioner of baseball told her that he was not in charge of hiring umpires.

Gera got a lawyer, Mario Biaggi, and filed a formal complaint with the Human Rights Commission. She contended, "There is no reason a woman cannot umpire a baseball game. It's just a matter of good eyesight, judgment, and ability to move around.

"I think I fit the qualifications better than most men."

After six years of legal battles, which commenced in 1969, the New York State Court of Appeals agreed with Gera's contention that established physical requirements for umpires were unjustified and discriminated against women.

She won that battle, but the war was still raging. When she went out to umpire her first game in June 1972, between the Auburn Phillies and the Geneva Rangers, Bernice told me that she was assailed with words like "bitch, cunt, whore" coming from everywhere. Certainly not an auspicious way to start.

Auburn club's Tony Ford was on second base with one out when John Dawkins hit a line drive at Rangers second baseman Jim Pascarella, who leaped and made the catch.

Geneva shortstop Brian Doyle and Ford were equidistant from second, and both raced to the bag; there both players and the ball arrived at about the same time. Gera signaled safe. The crowd howled, and Bernice changed her decision, calling Ford out. Nolan Campbell, manager of the Auburn Phillies, rushed onto the field and had the distinction of being the only manager thrown out of a professional baseball game by a female umpire.

Later Bernice said she had forgotten that a runner going into second base on an attempted double play did not have to be tagged and she had to change her call. She admitted that she had made a mistake on the first call. With the heavy emotions flying, Campbell told her she had made two mistakes. The first one was putting on a uniform. But then Campbell is not totally an innocent; the previous season he was thrown out nine times.

After the game was over, Bernice announced she was quitting. She told me she had other things on her mind. She was sick and suffering the aftereffects of a serious hepatitis episode that was debilitating. She had gotten what she wanted—if only for one day.

I think Gera was the trailblazer. In 1975 Christine Wren became baseball's second female umpire. She worked a short season in the Class A circuit, Northwest League. Apparently she did well and went on as far as the Midwest League in 1977. She quit when she found a better-paying job.

Now along comes Pam Postema. Although only twenty-eight she has been really honing up her umpiring skills in the minor leagues. In 1983 she had been promoted to the Pacific Coast League and became the first woman umpire to work at the Triple A level.

Postema was raised in Willard, Ohio, and at an early age she gave every evidence of being an excellent athlete. While enrolled at the University of Florida, she read an advertisement for the Al Somers Umpiring School in Daytona Beach, Florida. It probably seemed more interesting than some of her classes, and with the knowledge of her natural ability, she applied. Postema tried for six months to gain admittance before the school finally gave way, and she finished 17th out of the original class of 130.

I briefly shook her hand on a West Coast visit, but I am sure I'll see a lot more or her.

BACKSTAGE

Hoopla, hoopla! Baseball is about that too, and we love it. What's a circus without the stimulating foreplay, and what's baseball without its own charisma of a special kind?

From the time I was a little kid until this very moment, I can hardly wait to get into opening day at the ballpark. There's a special odor; an indefinable aura scents the air. The excitement is electric, and if you really love baseball, you'll succumb to it.

Every vendor has his own special pitch; I can see that little watery-eyed Irish guy with the reminiscence of a faint brogue standing there in his little white jacket and paper hat yelling, "Get your *Who's Who* in the major leagues here, here. A book with biogs and pictures of the ballplayers." He probably would have done well in a Madison Avenue advertising agency. Then off on the other side, you've got another guy, tall, scrawny, myopic but with a magnificent (if it can be) booming voice and obviously from the Bronx, sonorously screeching, "Get your scorecards here. You can't tell the players without a scorecard." Chills, thrills, expectations I have always had, and I hope it continues.

Opening day was like an anticipated concert with Duke Ellington or a great Broadway opening. Sometimes the concerts and plays left me feeling low, with an extrasad disappointment—but baseball never left me down.

121

*   *   *

Concessionairing is nothing new to baseball. Who wants to go to a party and bring your own food, drink, etc. You're on a holiday; you're not supposed to be encumbered with anything but pleasure.

In 1883 second baseman Joe Gerhardt of Louisville's major league American Association club took over part of a bar concession. It must have showed some potential because five years later Harry Raymond, third baseman of the same organization, managed to put extra money in his coffers from the sale of scorecards. The concept of the concessionaire took full flight when Harry M. Stevens became the first big-time entrepreneur in baseball.

As baseball grew into the realm of big business, so did the careers of the concessionaires. When I was a kid you could spend an especially pleasurable afternoon on a buck fifty. Hot dogs, 10 cents; sodas, 10 cents; peanuts, 5 cents; popcorn, 5 cents; scorecards, 10 cents; bleachers, 55 cents. A well-heeled day you eat in the grandstands, $1.10. But then everything is relative to the economy. Still, now it seems expensive for a large family to have to pay $2.00 for beer; $1.50 for a hot dog; and, really, Pepsi at $1.25.

I think back to those days when I attended the old Negro league games when they occurred in New York. The same white concessionaires serviced the white and Negro leagues then as well. It was all that some Black people could do to get to the game and pay the bleacher prices. They compromised on the purchase of baseball food and brought their home-cooked fried chicken and ham sandwiches and their own liquids. Nonetheless, they saw and enjoyed the game. The aroma of their picnic-style snacks made me heady. I would have gladly given up two frankfurters for a southern-fried chicken drumstick.

I think it's interesting to note that the frankfurter originated in Germany about 1852. The hot dog has become as indigenous to America as apple pie. Charles Feltman started the ball rolling. He was a vendor at Coney Island in about 1869. Business was bad, and he had to try and find a new way, a new product—anything, or he'd go under. Feltman found the frankfurter. And then he went one step further; he placed the hot dog in a roll. Instant success! By 1871 when ballplayers became truly professional, Charles Feltman already had his foot in the door. Harry M. Stevens bought Feltman's franks and hied his vendor troopers to the ballpark with hot water tanks loaded with this relatively new comestible; thus the birth of another American tradition (pizza pie looks as if it may rear its cheesy head at the games, though).

Then there was the hamburger. And like its name, it too was developed in Germany, but it, like most things, was probably conceived in the Baltic countries. A Dr. Salisbury, an American, obviously loved this food and introduced this "exotic" dish into the very plain American diet and called it the Salisbury steak. Some smart cookie put it on a bun and called it hamburger. It was easy selling. By 1912 the hamburger was on a par with the frankfurter (by then better known as the hot dog, a name designated by a newspaper reporter and cartoonist). The hamburger proved to be another ideal food for concessionaires. No forks or knives, easy.

Everything gets a curlicue or adapts to a particular cultural environment. In Honolulu's Aloha Stadium you may eat salmi (a Japanese noodle), manapua, and crock seed along with your hot dog and frankfurter. In addition you can have Chinese barbecued pork and green onions. Different strokes for different folks.

And then there were the peanuts. A big baseball seller, another "as American as apple pie." It's funny, though, to me peanuts were not just peanuts. Peanuts saved my male ego. Let me tell you about it. When I went to dear old P.S. 186, the only thing I heard about Black people was *Little Black Sambo*. To me he was a ludicrous character. All the pupils laughed at his ridiculous foibles, and in that context I felt I was placed. Embarrassed, ashamed, trust me, you got bad feelings. Even Tarzan in the Big Little Books made me cringe. Here was a white baboonlike man single-handedly able to conquer an entire tribe of fierce Black warriors. My people were portrayed as naked buffoons, cannibals (although I have since learned that cannibalism was not peculiar to the Black race but quite prevalent in Europe in ancient days). I used to recoil, sink, and slump in my seat when my white teacher in a predominantly white class would read these barbaric stories. It seemed that the responsibility to redeem my race had to be the reason for my existence.

In the third grade I had the good fortune to have Ms. Connie Evans as my teacher. Connie Evans was a Black woman, and in those days that was a rarity. But Connie Evans told us about George Washington Carver, an important Black scientist. Carver saved the economy of the South in the late 1800s by utilizing a peanut every way a peanut could be utilized. He made me proud, and I was thankful for him and Connie Evans.

However, then I went to George Washington High School. And after a gymnasium class this white guy and I were showering, changing clothes, and talking. I do not remember how, but some- how the talk got around to race. He said to me, "What have Negro people contributed to the world?" and I could only recall George Washington Carver. Out of utter frustration, I just punched him in the mouth. Sorry about that.

No one told me or taught me about Benjamin Banneker, who arranged and helped plan the city of Washington, D.C.; no one told me Blacks owned New York's famous Fraunces Tavern; no one taught me that the African Free Schools were the forerunners of the public education in New York; no one told me about the courageous runaway slave, Harriet Tubman, who led hundreds of Blacks out of southern slavery through the Underground Railroad. Who was to tell me that the first person killed in the American Revolution was Crispus Attucks, a Black freedman who believed in liberty? I didn't know about Dr. Daniel Hale Williams, a Black man who performed the first successful heart operation. Dr. Charles R. Drew was the leading authority on the preservation of blood plasma, directed the medical division of the British Blood Association, and during World War II worked with the American Red Cross as well as being the surgical consultant to the U.S. Army.

I never knew that the first American Negro poet to publish a volume of verse was a woman named Phyllis Wheatley, a Black slave. Dr. William A. Hinton of Harvard Medical School origi- nated the Hinton test for syphilis. Who told me about the Black congressmen who were *elected* to the Congress during the Reconstruction period and not dethroned until the advent of the Ku Klux Klan? Oh, boy, I was so ignorant.

I say all that to say that the vendors were the niggers of the ball clubs. They took their bruises and made money out of it.

Now peanuts were another thing. Peanuts and baseball go together, like Fred Astaire and Ginger Rogers.

There was a big rhubarb in Seals Stadium, San Francisco, in September 1950. Paul I. Fagan, president of the minor league Seals, announced that peanuts would not be sold because the cleanup job on the shells was costing the club $20,000 per season. This was far more than was obtained from the sale of the delicious little edibles. This did not bother the vendors because they anticipated reaping a harvest by selling peanuts outside of the park. Fans of all ages went on a rampage. They were determined to bring their own peanuts, eat them, and scatter the shells.

This tempest in a teapot continued. One man offered to supply the club with an electronic gadget guaranteed to detect concealed peanuts on customers. Seals' fans were breaking down the phones. Newspapers all over the country were printing the story. The *New York Times* asked its San Francisco representative for man-on-the-street interviews. Complaints were coming in from peanut growers and peanut-bag manufacturers.

President Fagan admitted defeat. He said, "I give up. Mr. Peanut wins. It's the first time in my life I've been beaten, and it had to be by a peanut." Fagan promised to give away eighteen thousand bags of peanuts free of charge to the fans.

But then in the middle of all of this, the boss of the janitors' union stated that the cleanup men would start to negotiate shortly with the San Francisco club for a raise from $1.35 to $1.50 an hour.

That was probably the end of the age of innocence in America.

I thank my lucky stars for the universality of baseball. The game cuts through all races, most religions, political persuasions, and professions.

I know that I am fortunate that doctors love baseball too. Those guys possibly saved my life. In August 1983 at Yankee Stadium Bobby Murcer's Day, I was one of the presenters for this auspicious occasion. The temperature had hit at least 90 degrees. On the field it must have been over 100. My doctor, Richard Fried, had put me on hypertension pills about two days before. Granted it was hot as hell on the field. I got back to the dugout, and the world became heady. I looked at Yankee manager Billy Martin and said, "Hey, man, I don't feel so good." Billy looked at me and said, "Art, you look all right." Then I felt as if someone were throwing a curtain around me. In my last recognition of consciousness, I thought, "Oh my God—the big ball orchard in the sky."

But in the meantime Dr. John Bonamo and trainer Gene Monahan were working over me like astronauts on a space flight. I credit them with possibly saving my life. The next thing I remembered was awakening in an ambulance heading for Lenox Hill Hospital. It was a brief episode, but it could have been fatal. So I'm glad and happy that there are addicted doctors and trainers who watch out for your physical transgressions.

I always have mixed emotions about doctors. It comes down to a love/hate mixture. They are supreme, or they are stupid. I've run into both kinds, and thankfully I have managed to survive with that crude a mixture.

But there have been doctors I have revered. I can see "Doc" Weaver now—short with silvery white hair walking out of the Polo Grounds team visitors' clubhouse. Instinctively, I knew he cared. There was this warmth that I had when I saw his silver wire glasses surrounding the top of his round face.

But the funny thing is that Doc Harrison Weaver wasn't really a doctor but a trainer for the St. Louis Cardinals. I have to give deference and respect to doctors because of the arduous training they have to endure, but on the baseball field give me Doc Weaver.

Oh my God, I can see him now. In a previous life he must have been a witch doctor or voodoo doctor, something like that. This onetime Ohio Wesleyan fullback used to give the Yankees the double whammy in spades, diamonds, hearts, and clubs.

I'd see him stare out at the Yankee team from the dugout in the 1942 World Series, wiggle his thumb and index fingers and gesticulate at the players. Surprisingly, the Yanks succumbed to this magic that Weaver perpetrated.

In a counterreaction, the Yankees let loose "Doc" Painter, a trainer for thirteen years, to sport his peculiar and particular weave of magic.

Then everybody got into the act, it seems. Art Fletcher, the Yankee coach, stopped the game because Butch Yatkeman, the Cardinals' veteran clubhouse man, was sending out pointed signals with his fingers to put the whammy on the Yankees.

Ah, such marvelous, fine madness.

My father had great respect for Dr. Robert Hyland, St. Louis Cardinal team physician. All I could remember about Dr. Hyland was that he was always performing a bone chip operation on one of the Cardinal pitchers.

I laughed so much when my father told me the story about Cardinal right-hander Tex Carleton (1933). He was losing so much weight the club was concerned about him and his health. Dr. Hyland examined him, could not find anything wrong with him. Dr. Hyland recommended that Carleton should have two or three strong highballs before dinner each night. Prohibition was still in effect at that time, and Doc Hyland had to leave a prescription for Carleton to be able to carry the whiskey on the road.

It is saddening to me that at this time we have to worry about the hard drugs and steroids that our idols procure and assimilate to use for what they think makes them better performers.

But then don't we always do that? This human race has invented its own demons. There are legends about fire-snorting dragons, deities that flow from heaven above who will enrich and enhance our shallow little lives. We take all this guff—but the smart ones make a business of it, get rich, and say, "Devil take the hind parts."

Witch doctors, high priests (and, for women's liberation, high priestesses), fooled everybody. But sometimes they saw the inner being that exists in all of us.

All the supermen are out there one way or the other. You have to take one-time New York Yankee trainee Gus Mauch. He is one of those with the special talent, whatever it might be. But he had the sparkle, the spunkles, that made the dream a reality. Oh my God, I wish there were more men of this ilk. Where the hell are they hiding? Come out, come out, wherever you are.

God bless the women and God bless my positive reaction to them: my mother, my aunts, my wife, my daughter. They have taught me a thing or two. I will never disrespect anyone because they are of a different gender because we are all only human beings.

The woman's liberation movement made me shudder when I became totally cognizant of the unfair, unrealistic posture man had taken toward females for whatever men had fathomed.

I have had too much love for women, and I don't mean promiscuity, to defame any efforts they employ to declare their equality. That is why I cheer those women who in the 1880s wore their flowing skirts and played a series of exhibition games at Philadelphia, New York, and Newark.

I am sure the ridicule they received was tantamount to being the fat lady in the circus or the elephant man. Shame on us.

Baseball was no strange thing to women, which was certainly an indication of their ability to understand and appreciate a complex kind of chess game. I don't know why men didn't recognize this more quickly, but as they say, "too old too smart or too smart too old."

I regret having so little to say. Maybe I have not researched enough or maybe the qualms of the times have not produced enough, or, if, either, I, etc., etc., etc., or maybe it's just portents of things to come. God! I hope I'm not a toothless codger looking at film of Joe DiMaggio smacking baseballs all over the ball orchard, or a Dwight Gooden hurtling the sphere over 95 miles per hour over home plate before women reach their proper niche.

I never anticipated it as a "stickball" kid, but I assuredly recognized the positive reality of it.

In 1890 the first all-women team was formed. Of course they had played baseball and enjoyed sports before they could even consider organizing a team, but they were considered merely an amusing diversion. The women coiled or braided their hair and went out on the field with the gusto of an all-male ball club. The

BACKSTAGE

"Young Ladies Baseball Club No. 1," I read, played in competition with some male clubs and handled themselves competently. The lineup of the Young Ladies Baseball Club read like this:

W. S. Franklin, Manager
May Howard, Pitcher . . . Captain
Nellie Williams, Catcher
Katie Grant, First Base
Angie Parker, Second Base
Edith Mayres, Third Base
Effie Earl, Shortstop
Alice Lee, Third Base
Rose Mitchell, Right Field
Annie Grant, Center Field

Seldom do you read about or much less hear about these spunky women who defied the historical frieze they were locked into.

And then in the early 1900s the Bloomer Girls emerged. They were a popular attraction, and despite the name, at least three males were in the starting lineup. Yes, fans lined up to see them, but it was just an amusing triple.

Bill Compton, the third baseman, was called Dolly Madison. The pitcher, a male, was called Lady Waddell. Joe Wood, who had a Michael Jackson type of face, and an alternate varying number of young males went out there donning wigs and probably yelled, "Let's play ball." Ah, the game, it crosses so many divergencies of our society.

Hall of Famer Rogers Hornsby's big stint was on a bloomer girls team. It couldn't be that bad, right!

In reading about it, thinking about it, I recognized or foresaw the inevitability in a change of mores. Though I would like to think that I'm a wise man, I am not. However, you'd have to be hit over the head not to be cognizant of the fact that women were preparing to come out of the proverbial closet: "Here I come, ready or not."

And then I read about this young fifteen-year-old girl, Amanda Clement of Hudson, South Dakota, who could throw a ball 275 feet.

She stood behind the plate at age fifteen and umpired a men's baseball game (first known woman umpire). Tough cookie for

1903, and a breakthrough that gave portents of different things to come.

There are probably a fantastic number of competent, unheralded females who have participated in the sport of baseball, but certain names stick out. Ah, but there was one splendid athlete that I perchance saw, Babe Didrikson Zaharias.

Only through constant reading have I learned that she gained national prominence as a basketball player. This lady from Dallas, Texas, excelled in every sport she sought to conquer: hurling the javelin; golf. As a teenager she was nominated for three all-American teams and even once scored 106 points in a basketball game.

A kind of peculiar energy seemed to invade her body. Of the 634 track and field events in which she was entered, Babe won all but 12. At golf she won the U.S. Amateur title in 1946, the British Amateur title in 1947, and the Women's Professional titles in 1948, 1950, and 1954.

Then this Babe went on to pitch for the House of David, a trumped-up Midwestern religious cult baseball team. I happened to see her perform at the Polo Grounds with this club, and I was truly amazed at how hard she could throw a baseball. The House of David wore the mandatory beards of Orthodox Jews, but the bulk of them were not. They were just another version of an amusement park attraction. They only rivaled Negro league teams in their preposterous behavior and often opposed them in exhibiton games as they barnstormed across the country.

In this mélange of buffoonery why not hire a woman pitcher? The obvious is clear—Babe Didrikson. For one year she barnstormed with them.

She was a good pitcher, but she didn't get her fair share. The Babe was treated like a woman and not like an equal competitor. The opposing team wouldn't bunt on her or hit a line drive through the box, fearing they would injure her.

The House of David used her as dressing, and they'd only pitch her two or three innings and take her out because she was often good enough to strike out the opposing team, and they would possibly seek vengeance, and believing in male physical superiority,

they were trying to protect her. But I think Babe could have pro-
tected herself competently against a mass murderer.

In 1943 the All-American Girls Baseball League was initiated
by the then Chicago Cubs owner Phil Wrigley. This Midwestern
league lasted twelve seasons. Its popularity was drawn from the
fact that World War II was still on. The availability of your superstar male players had been diverted to the military.

Nonetheless, the All-American Girls Baseball League had six
active teams. You had the Fort Wayne Daisies, the Milwaukee
Chicks, the South Bend Blue Sox, the Kenosha Comets, the
Racine Belles, and the Rockford Peaches. Mostly foolishly chau-
vinistic titles; however, these women had the ability.

For the ladies I say "yea" for the courage of trying and perhaps
in that new dawn acoming things may be a bit different.

There is no way I can leave out one of my favorite people—
Eddie Layton, organist at Madison Square Garden and the Yankee
Stadium.

Eddie's a very introspective, sensitive person, and besides, how
many New Yorkers own a tugboat? That's style.

When I get to the Yankee Stadium and we're eating in the press-
room, I suggest to him what I'd like to hear him play that day. It's
usually some 1930s–'40s sentimental but beautiful song that reminds me of my parents—*Deep Purple* or *My Reverie*. Damn if
Eddie doesn't play it before the night is over.

Eddie has a snag too, but it is in good humor and easily acceptable. A bit of ethnicity sets in when Cerone or any Italian ballplayer comes to the plate. Eddie will play a tarantella. A Polish
player will probably get a polka.

One day when Dave Winfield came up, I warned him not to play
"Swanee River." All of us around him fell out laughing, and it's
nice to be mirthful because sometimes that can put things in their
rightful perspective.

Eddie conjures up wonderful memories. But memories are nothing but preparations for the present and expectations of the future.

Thank you, Eddie Layton.

SOME ROADS LEAD TO COOPERSTOWN: THE GREATEST BALLPLAYERS THESE FOUR EYES HAVE EVER SEEN

To someone who doesn't know, it is very hard to explain the magic, the intensity that baseball exudes. It has been the woof and weave that has constituted my life.

My first love was the St. Louis Cardinals in general (undoubtedly my father's influence). There was something special about this club that I could not define in my early youth but later through reading and experience I grew to understand.

Originally the St. Louis Cardinals were the Cleveland Spiders. The owner, Frank De Haas Robison, a tractor magnate, had the Spiders. In 1898 the Spider franchise was transferred to St. Louis because Robison felt that Cleveland had not appreciated his efforts or supported his club as well as he felt the franchise warranted. St. Louis, Missouri, was the most well populated sports-loving city west of the Alleghenies. Hungry for sports and any kind of cultural development, St. Louis was an unusual city. After the Civil War, it became the principal distribution point for the Mississippi Valley. It acquired its prominence as a wholesale and manufacturing center. This was a town with money to burn and would easily welcome a winning ball club.

Robison was one of those freewheeling, free-spending guys that typified the American "go get it" philosophy. St. Louis was a town of tough, crude nouveau riche and hard to handle. A club like the Cleveland Spiders, also tough, crude, and "gutsy," would inspire a city like St. Louis to say "come on," and so they did.

When the almost intact club transferred to the St. Louis franchise and became the St. Louis Cardinals, this hard-rock crew who came down from Cleveland germinated, went through a process of maturation, catapulting as one of the most exciting ball clubs around.

Sure, the guys were bawdy, scrambling, and "I don't give a damn" attitudinally, but they played the game and that was what you were paying for. By the late 1930s they were formidable, almost like unleashed Doberman pinschers waiting for the enemy. I loved them. My father saw something in them that was special—a kind of fierce determination that had made America America.

The Great Depression was in full force then, and perhaps subliminally we took courage from this team that didn't give in to anything. At least that is what I thought at that time.

And so these tough hooligans of diverse backgrounds became my heroes. Sure, the Yankees were great, but they had all the opportunities. I wanted my Ganghouse Gang—the survivors of any disaster.

But the main person I identified with was Joseph Michael "Ducky Wucky" Medwick. His career was the typically phenomenal American success story. He was born November 24, 1911. His parents were Hungarian immigrants who finally settled in Carteret, New Jersey. Joe Medwick was the American dream. He had participated in every sport. There is no doubt that he was a gifted athlete. Even in his freshman year at high school he was an all-state in football, basketball, and baseball. Definitely a "triple threat performer." Notre Dame tried to ferret him from high school, but he was deficient in 1½ credits for admission and honestly didn't feel like attending prep school to acquire them.

After finishing high school in 1929, he played for Scottdale, Pennsylvania, in the Middle Atlantic League. He used the name Mickey King to protect his amateur status in the event that he might attend college. Joe batted .419 with 100 RBIs (runs batted in) in 75 games, and he was only eighteen years old.

With his extraordinary performance he was picked up and became a great favorite with the Houston Buffs in the Texas League in 1931. He led the league in home runs as well as runs batted in, and he also picked up the nickname Ducky Wucky. All our heroes have chinks in their armor, and Joseph Medwick had his. A woman fan said he walked like a duck, and perhaps he did, but nevertheless he was dubbed Ducky Wucky his entire career. Of course he didn't like the appellation, but when he was able to share in the proceeds of the Ducky Wucky candy bar, there were no more verbal protests from him.

And this was long before Reggie Jackson's Reggie bar became a comestible bar of candy.

But then I identify with Joe in more ways than one. There comes that particular time when you want to grow up; when you want to feel independent and separate unto yourself. Well, my way was to go to the ball games alone in an effort, I suppose, to assert my ability to control and master my own maturation and prepare for the life that I knew was coming.

In my wild assessment of my coming manhood, I latched onto a hero: You guessed it, Ducky Wucky. The fear was there in a ten-year-old kid traveling alone, but I braved it. Autograph book in hand, I approached Joe Medwick. Firstly, of course, I admired his awesome skill, but to see him in leaving the Polo Grounds in his splendiferous sartorial attire was another thing. I see it all so clearly—a tan linen suit, Panama straw hat, and brown-and-white spectator shoes and a brown-and-white polka-dotted tie. Seemingly draped over his arm was a magnificently beautiful blond wife, a definned mermaid. I asked for his autograph, and he so graciously responded I knew he would be my idol forever. His dress, his stance, the generosity poured from him and so reminded me of my father. Ridiculously, foolishly, I wanted to cry when he asked my name to sign the book.

IRVING RUST

Arthur was a nut about Medwick. Arthur used to lift up his left leg the same way Medwick did before he hit the baseball. Arthur even wore his baseball cap low-browed, pinched bill, as did Medwick.

It's so long ago, but I don't think Art ever took off the

pinched-bill cap for the summer. Somehow I think Medwick had impressed him.

He even had a portrait of Medwick emblazoned and Scotch-taped upon his wall, despite the fact that it was from the back of the Wheaties box.

But there was so much more to Medwick. He definitely was someone to admire for his specific talents. The 1937 National League triple crown winner with a .374 batting average; he led the league in runs batted in with 154 and tied Mel Ott of the Giants in homers with 31; he also led in runs scored, 111; hits 237; total bases 407; and doubles with 56. How can you not love a champion like that? And despite the fact that the National League lost the 1937 All-Star game in Washington 8–3, Medwick crashed 4 hits for the losers; but then baseball is a team sport, and every member has his responsibility. Nonetheless, Medwick was voted the most valuable player of the National League in 1937.

Medwick also had a temper as hot as Mount Vesuvius and was a back-talking, stubborn mule of a man, as my father told me, but you had to admire his courage.

My father often speaks of the seventh game of the 1934 World Series between the St. Louis Cardinals and the Detroit Tigers. During the Cardinals 7-run third inning, Joe Medwick hit a 3 bagger, and as he slid into third base, he had an altercation with Marvin Owen, the Tiger third baseman. Owen didn't like the way Medwick came into the bag, and Medwick thought Owen put the ball on him with unnecessary roughness. Heated words were exchanged, a few wild swings, but Bill Klem, the third-base umpire, prevented any real fisticuffs.

As things grew bleaker and bleaker for Detroit, the Tiger fans, especially the left field bleacher occupants, worked themselves into an ugly mood. Most of their resentment was directed against Medwick. They clobbered him with vegetables, fruit, scorecards, pop bottles, anything the fans could get their hands on. Several times the field was clear, only to have a fresh variety burst from the stands.

The crowd chanted of Medwick . . . "Take him out! Take him

out!'' The chant echoed and reechoed like a football yell. Tiger pilot Mickey Cochrane ran halfway into left field and attempted pacification of the crowd with one gesture, to no avail. The umpires milled about helplessly.

Umpires and players pleaded with the crowd to cease throwing edibles, but their pleas fell on deaf ears. It got so bad in the seventh inning that Medwick couldn't take his regular position. Judge Landis then called a meeting with Medwick, Owen, and the umpires in his box. The judge asked Medwick to leave the game, and Cardinal manager Frankie Frisch assigned Chick Fullis to left field. Landis said he took this action ''to protect the player from injury and permit the game to proceed.'' However, many at the Series felt this was not one of the commissioner's best decisions.

When Medwick's batting average fell off 52 points in 1938 from his 1937 high, Cardinal president Sam Breadon reduced Joe's contract by $2,000. Medwick was a holdout well into spring training and was disgruntled much of the year. The St. Louis fans got an idea he wanted to get out of the Mound City, possibly to follow his good buddy Leo Durocher to Brooklyn.

Then, in June of 1940, with his popularity declining, in one of the biggest trades of that era, Joe was sent to Brooklyn to play for his pal Durocher.

The Dodgers faced the St. Louis Cardinals on June 19, 1940, in the second game of a series in Ebbets Field. The day before the Cardinals had won and knocked Brooklyn out of first place. They also held Medwick hitless, and needled the hell out of him.

I remember the next day so completely. With my father and my Crosley radio and great intensity, we listened to Red Barber report this exciting event. Dixie Walker, Cookie Lavagetto, and Joe Vosmick hit safely in the first inning. Bob Bowman was on the mound, and Ducky Wucky was at the plate.

Bowman sent a mean pitch high and light; Medwick was hit behind the ear. The velocity and inherent speed of the pitch knocked Medwick to the ground. There was a near riot on the field. The ferocious and unnecessary encounter infuriated the fans. The situation instigated an investigation by William O'Dwyer, then district attorney in Brooklyn. Although the investigation absolved Bowman of any charges, it led to the development of a suitable batting helmet.

When Medwick returned from the hospital after suffering a concussion, blurred vision, and earaches, fans thought he was plate shy, and who the hell wouldn't be—a burned child fears the fire. It matters not whatever the cause, Medwick was never again to attain the greatness that he had had with St. Louis, despite the fact that he hit .300 or better for the next three years.

In 1943 he was traded to the Giants, and he remained with them until 1945. Thereafter he was sent to the Boston Braves. I continued to follow his career because of the special man that he was; however, I thought to myself how demoralizing it must be to be handled like a piece of beef. By 1946 he was again with the Dodgers. He joined them in time for their stretch run against the Cardinals, who won the pennant in a playoff.

You know the slogan "Old soldiers never die." That's the nice part to remember, but don't forget the coda, "they just fade away." Medwick went to the camp in 1947, and he was at camp with the New York Yankees, but they released him. Curtains! Career was over as far as Medwick was concerned. But no, you don't throw good meat away. Cardinal owner Sam Breadon requested that Medwick rejoin the club as a pinch hitter and a part-time player.

Medwick was sitting on the bench observing the first game between the Cards and the Pirates on one of those great days in May. It was the fifth inning of the second game; the score was 2–0 with the Cardinals trailing. Such excitement! Manager Eddie Dyer looked over to the bench when the Cardinals got a man at first. Dyer had the faith. He looked Medwick dead in the eye and said, "You're the hitter."

Medwick was probably defecating bullets, but did whatever was necessary. Fritz Ostermueller was on the mound for Pittsburgh, and he ran the count 2 and 1 on Ducky. Medwick reached out and lined a shot to right center field, driving in the Cardinals' only run. The tears flowed freely in St. Louis that day.

Medwick played out the 1947 season in St. Louis and then appeared in a few games in 1948 before taking over as manager of the Houston Buffs of the Texas League for three seasons, then retiring from baseball in 1952.

Medwick was elected to baseball's Hall of Fame in 1968.

Joseph Michael Ducky Wucky Medwick will always be an integral part of my baseball life.

As much as I loved Medwick, I had another hero. The Yankee Clipper, Joseph Paul DiMaggio. He was the eighth of nine children born to Giuseppe and Rosalie DiMaggio. His parents had emigrated from Isola della Femmina, a small island off the coast of Sicily. They migrated to America and remained for a short time in New York before they settled in San Francisco.

Actually Joe grew up in the streets around Fisherman's Wharf. His father made his living as a fisherman, but Joe never cottoned to that kind of career. He started playing baseball in an area called the Horse Lot, because a milk company let them use it if they rounded up the horses resting on it. It was an easy thing to do, since his brothers were avid fans and amateur players, and it beat fishing. Joe always considered his older brother Tom the greatest ballplayer, but perhaps the time was not right. I didn't know Tom's skill, but I did see his brother Vince, who broke in with the Boston Bees in 1937, and his older brother Dominic, who started with the Boston Red Sox in 1940. I think that brother was as equally a defensive genius as his brother Joe.

Well, anyway, when he was still a long-legged kid Joe played ball at the Horse Lot, the bases were concrete blocks and home plate was a flattened oilcan. When I read about this, it recalled my childhood with sewer tops as bases.

DiMag's professional career began in 1932 when his brother Vince was an outfielder with the San Francisco Seals of the Pacific Coast League. It was the last week of the season when Augie Galan wanted to bypass the last 3 games so that he could go to Hawaii with Henry "Prince" Oana, an outfielder with the Seals. That left San Francisco manager Ike Caveney manager without a shortstop. Vince suggested that he try his kid brother Joe, and he was in.

At Joe's first turn at the plate, he clubbed a triple off the left field wall. It is interesting to note that although Joe basically played shortstop, it was as a hitter of home runs that he was increasing his fame.

When Joe reported to the San Francisco training camp the following spring, Seals' owner Charley Graham watched him work out in the infield, then signed him for $250 a month.

DiMaggio wasn't able to beat out Augie Galan at shortstop, so he rode the bench and pinch-hit for a couple of weeks.

Finally manager Caveney moved DiMaggio to right field.

In that 1933 season, Joe hit safely in 61 consecutive games, breaking the 49-game record skein set by first baseman Jack Ness of the Oakland Oaks in 1915.

During that skein, Caveney moved Joe into the leadoff position in the batting order to afford him extra chances, but Oakland stopped him on July 26, after he had hit safely in 61 straight. Joe batted .340 that season. Charley Graham realized he had a tiger by the tail and seriously listened to sale offers about this valuable player. However, and by whatever powers may be, Joe's left knee gave way completely, the tendons were torn and he was out of the lineup for weeks. In June 1934, after a long doubleheader and then dinner at a married sister's house, Joe rode home in a cramped taxi and his left leg became numb. When he put his foot on the pavement, he heard something pop.

This was the first in a long period of injuries that haunted his career. The leg injury affected his career by withdrawal or the slowing down of his salability. Graham had been asking major league ball clubs to give him $70,000 for the purchase of Joe's talent. Their reluctance, because of the questionable leg, dropped the price considerably—damaged goods go cheaper.

Yankee scouts Joe Devine and Vinegar Bill Essick looked at Joe and still recommended the purchase. This had to be one of the greatest bargains in history: $25,000. The Yankees agreed to let him remain with the Seals in 1935. Jolting Joe reported to the Yankees in St. Petersburg in February 1936 for spring training.

Joe DiMaggio's greatest hit was full force in 1936 when he joined the Yankees. Ah, the reveries conjured up by that period of time when life was simple. I thank God for the peace and tranquility my parents afforded me. I didn't know there was a Depression and people were hungry, jobless—everything was hunky-dory with me, and perhaps that was wrong, but I knew no different. Somehow Joe DiMag combined with that special spirit. I saw him frequently, and I grew to love some of his principal traits; the grace and the elegance on the baseball diamond. Joe made everything look so easy, which of course is the mark of a true champion.

Well, I recall the first time I saw him. It was the latter part of August 1936. There was a Tournament of Champions Day at the Yankee Stadium. The Yankees played the Cleveland Indians in a regularly scheduled contest.

But part of the entertainment that day was the House of David baseball team, who competed against the New York Fire Department baseball team. That was a four-inning exhibition game.

On top of that they had four–gold–medal–winner Black Jesse Owens fresh back from the Olympic games in Berlin. He too was another hero of mine; however, in retrospect, I don't think his skills, courage, and determination should have been directed toward racing a horse—something demeaning in that; would Mark Spitz have had to race or compete with a shark?

Onetime baseball player Al Schacht became a baseball clown. His antics that day doubled me up in laughter. But Joe, Joe, Jolting Joe DiMaggio, you captured my spirit and enthusiasm that day, and it has never left me—Joe DiMaggio—an aristocrat in pinstripes.

SONNY CURTIS

Arthur used to confuse me when we were playing on St. Nicholas Avenue.

One day he was Joe Medwick, another day he was Mel Ott, but after a while he was mostly Joe DiMaggio.

Although Joe missed 16 games in his 1936 rookie season because of a burn sustained while undergoing diathermy treatment, he tied for the league lead in triples with 15, hit 44 doubles and 29 homers among 206 hits. He also drove in 125 runs and batted .323.

In Joe's initial season the Yankees won the pennant by 19½ games.

The Yankees were soaring, and so were my feelings. I didn't think it was an accident that the Yankees started their run of four consecutive pennants when Joe joined the club. During his thirteen years' tenure the Yankees won ten pennants, and you can blame it all on DiMaggio.

In 1939 I was sitting in the bleachers at the Yankee Stadium with Georgie Vaz and Roy Cobb when I witnessed one of the greatest catches I ever saw in my life. There was Joe D racing back to center field. He got behind the flagpole and the monuments at the 461-foot mark; he turned, gyrated, and gloved the ball hit by Detroit's Hank Greenberg a second before he hit the fence. My friends, I tell you, that was geometry and ballet, and that's probably how the pyramids were built. (Don't you wonder how the hell they did that?) The only thing, though, was that after that spectacular catch, the Yankee Clipper seemed to have forgotten that the catch hadn't retired the side, and his teammates were screaming for the ball to attempt to double up a runner who was trying to retrace his steps from third to first.

Never, never, never will I forget Joe's 56-game hitting streak in 1941. I ate, slept, and drank it. All the guys on St. Nicholas Avenue were completely caught up in the excitement of this rather taciturn, seemingly aloof man who expended what appeared to be his life's energy in hitting that ball. It made me delirious. Now that I'm considerably older, I wonder what is the chemistry that makes this so wonderful, fulfilling, and wondrous. Perhaps it's in the improbability that we find a way to conquer the exigencies and uncertainties of our existence. Joe D found a way, and it gave everyone hope. That's good enough!

"Chump," the guy who delivered ice for Tony, and at least seven years older than we were, idolized DiMaggio, and perhaps it gave him courage doing that crummy job.

For two months and 56 consecutive games, DiMaggio got at least one hit in each contest. This was a phenomenal achievement that was considered a coup and probably the most incredible offensive accomplishment in big league baseball's first century.

The streak was such a fantastic revelation. It could be done. If you are as old as I am, I dreamed of a man walking on the moon, but Joe D showed me that everything is possible.

On July 17 at Cleveland the most talked-about baseball happening came to an end. I heard Mel Allen do this game on radio by way of the Western Union ticker and hung on every pitch. That night off Indian lefty Al Smith, Joe hit two screamers that were fielded brilliantly by Cleveland third baseman Kenny Keltner. Once DiMaggio walked. In the eighth inning, facing right-hander Jim Bagby, Joe hit one of the ultimate ground smashes of his career, but the ball was grabbed by the deft shortstop Lou Boudreau, who started a double play that ended the skein.

DiMaggio went out the next day and started another consecutive game run. He hit in 16 more games.

In those 56 games, DiMaggio had 91 hits, which included 16 doubles, 4 triples, and 15 homers, for 160 total bases. He drove in 55 runs, walked 21 times, and struck out just seven of 223 times at bat.

During his batting streak, Joseph Paul meant enough for a popular disc jockey, Allen Courtney, to pen the words to a song on a nightclub tablecloth. Courtney showed the poem to Les Brown, leader of the Band of Renown. In turn Brown gave the lyrics to writer Ben Homer, who gave the lyrics a tune and a lift, and it was so good in those troubled times:

> *Who started baseball's famous streak*
> *That's got us all aglow?*
> *He's just a man and not a freak*
> *Jolting Joe DiMaggio*
> *Joe . . . Joe . . . DiMaggio . . . We*
> *Want you on our side.*
>
> *From coast to coast, that's all you hear*
> *Of Joe the one-man show.*
> *He's glorified the horsehair's sphere*
> *Jolting Joe DiMaggio*
> *Joe . . . Joe . . . DiMaggio . . . We*
> *Want you on our side.*
>
> *He'll live in baseball's Hall of Fame*

RECOLLECTIONS OF A BASEBALL JUNKIE

He got there blow by blow
Our kids will tell their kids his name,
Jolting Joe DiMaggio.

I was fresh out of college in the latter part of June 1949. I rewarded the victory of my receiving my B.S. degree by journeying to Boston to see DiMaggio play his first game of the season. Unfortunately he had had to miss the first 65 games of the schedule. Joe had had an operation on his right heel for the removal of painful bone spurs that winter, and his recuperation period was necessarily lengthy.

It matters, and it matters not; Joe in a 3-game set-to with the Boston Red Sox displayed one of the greatest offensive shows in the history of baseball. Awesome! In those contests Joe hit 4 home runs, batted in 9, and scored 5 and led the Yankees to a 3-game sweep. His performance was out of a J. Arthur Rank movie.

I have had the privilege of meeting Joe D many times since his last major league season in 1951. To me he has appeared to be a quietly reflective man, marching to his own drummer.

I considered Joe D the acme of perfection and without question the greatest player I ever saw. There's a special kind of emotion here that evokes a period of my life that was relatively uncomplicated. Joe emits the same mystical and extraordinary power that Nat King Cole exuded. It was a semblance of early manhood, family, strict adherence to the code of friendship. I don't know how, what, or why, but I grew up with Joe D. He was a chunk of my life.

But I was not alone. There were millions of Americans who identified with the spirit of the man. It was World War II, and perhaps all of us needed Joe for courage and at least diversion. We knew Joe could beat the unbeatable foe.

If you're lucky, heroes come in multiple numbers; therefore, perhaps you have a choice. The 5'9" Littlest Giant Mel Ott thrilled me to my toes. How many times did I see him pop one down the 257-foot right field line for a round-tripper at the Polo Grounds? He was sweet. He was the elusive dream that we all pursue.

Ott was born March 2, 1909, in Gretna, way down in the bayou

146

territory of Louisiana. A natural from the get-go—high school football, basketball, as well as baseball; but baseball was his major thing. He had had a special entree because his father and uncle had been fairly successful semipro ballplayers. But then don't so many things start and germinate that way. A father's expectations just may incite a child to extend and supercede the challenges that a parental figure may evoke.

At the age of sixteen, Ottie, as he was affectionately called, traveled to New Orleans with his high school batterymate Lester Ruprich and had the audacity to ask the owner of the Southern Association's New Orleans Pelicans for a job. They hired Ruprich, who was three years older than Ott, and said words tantamount to get lost to the latter because he was "too small and too young." As most sixteen-year-old kids who are rejected, Ott was down and out, when, with the compassion of an older man, Alex Heineman, owner of the New Orleans Pelicans, told the youngster that if he really wanted to play, perhaps he could work out a deal where he would be hired with a semipro team, the Patterson Braves, where they played only 3 or 4 times a week. Patterson, Louisiana, was the answer, 90 miles from New Orleans.

Harry Williams, a rich sportsman, was the man he was to meet. Williams gave Ott a job playing baseball at $150 a month plus expenses. Not bad for a sixteen-year-old kid in those days, and the expenses included movies, sodas, and haircuts—perhaps paradise for a sixteen-year-old country boy.

Everything went well, and although offered a Southern Association contract from Heineman at New Orleans, Ott was not allowed to accept it by Williams, who had a "morality" agreement. A bit embittered, Ott felt he was slated to play on a "down home" club the rest of his baseball career, that is, the Patterson Braves.

Then out of the blue Ott received a postcard from his original patron, Williams, sent from New York on his return form abroad. The card read "Report to John McGraw at the Polo Grounds for a tryout on September 1." Of course, Ott did not believe it and ignored its implication. When Williams returned to Patterson, he was appalled to find Mel still catching for the Patterson Braves.

Posthaste, Williams bought Mel Ott a train ticket to New York, and so with his little straw suitcase he managed to reach the Big Apple.

Again the sagacious McGraw, given the greater part of wisdom, granted his good friend Williams his judgment. With trepidation he took on the sturdy sixteen-year-old youngster.

McGraw did not know what to think about this boy/man, but the books indicate that it was negative.

And then one morning he was at the park early, and he saw someone hitting the ball so hard and so well in practice he queried someone and found out that this was the "kid" that his friend Williams had recommended. McGraw, that sly devil, had a good eye and saw the possible potential value of this very young man. What McGraw saw was a natural, and perhaps an inbred natural swinger, who had the grasp, the feel, the intelligence, the intuitiveness to be something. Ottie was to be definitively contracted to the Giants.

And then the chips fell where they should. Ott was most unusual for his distinctive batting stance. He was a left-handed swinger. Visualize this: He planted his feet far apart, and then he raised his right leg to knee height while the pitcher was preparing to deliver the ball. The anticipation was excruciatingly painful. Then Ott planted the right foot on the ground again just before impact with the pitch. The swing was a good level stroke. Genius!

Despite his high kick at the plate, Ott could not be pitched to. Ott being a pull hitter, the short right field wall at the Polo Grounds was dessert for him.

At the age of seventeen Ott struck out the first time at bat in 1926, although only batting 60 times. He ran off 5 straight pinch hits before he failed twice in succession. I don't think that's bad for a seventeen-year-old kid. At the end of the season, he had appeared in 35 games, but nonetheless his batting average was .383 and would be the highest average of his baseball career.

Mel made his first big league home run against the Chicago Cubs in the 1927 season in New York. God, I wish I had seen it instead of just hearing about it. Mel got into 82 contests and batted .282. His only homer came on a drive on which Hack Wilson slipped in mud and the ball hopped past him for an inside-the-park home run.

SOME ROADS LEAD TO COOPERSTOWN

I was caught up in the excitement of the man in 1933. He seemed to be all my father and my uncle Johnny talked about. Ottie was definitely the star of the Giants in the 1933 World Series against the Washington Senators. The first game, the first inning an error by Buddy Myer at second put Jo-Jo Moore on first and brought up Ottie, who promptly crushed a 400-foot home run off Senator left-hander Walter Stewart. That shot stood up for a 4–2 win for Carl Hubbell, who was aided further by a run-scoring single by Ott. In his first World Series at the age of twenty-four, Master Melvin went 4 for 4.

Ott won the last game of the '33 Series just as he had the first but even more dramatically. In inning number ten of that contest at Griffith Stadium, with the score tied, he hit a long drive to center field where Fred Schulte went back and leaped. The ball bounced off Schulte's glove and into the temporary bleachers and disappeared among the fans. It was first called a ground-rule double by the umpires and, after vehement Giant protestations, was reversed and called a home run. Ott's blow gave the Giants a 4–3 victory and the World Championship.

As a home run slugger, Mel was indeed favored by the short right field barrier at the Polo Grounds, where he hit 323 of his 511 homers. I saw many of those round-trippers and the last one, which occurred opening day in 1946. Ott hit a home run his first time up against Philadelphia Phillie Oscar Judd.

Absolutely no one who was around baseball in the 1930s or '40s could ever forget the graceful style, on or off the field, of Mel Ott. I mean there was no way you could diminish a man who had hit 511 homers and had a lifetime record of .304, knocking in 1,860 runs as well as having to play that right field wall at the Polo Grounds. That is incredible skill, and I give it its rightful due.

I love "stand-up" guys, and I try to emulate their special qualities to the best of my abilities.

In 1942 when Bill Terry stepped down from the Giant helm, Ott became the player-manager with the ball club. He was the field boss until 1948, when he was fired and replaced by Leo Durocher.

After the Giants let him go, Ott remained as a scout and broadcaster.

On November 21, 1958, Melvin Thomas Ott, a chunk of my life, died after an automobile accident.

When I think back to all my idols, I feel like Ali Baba—I found the cave, the chest of jewels, marveled, and without the forty thieves. Well, another hero comes up—Carl Hubbell. He was long, lean, gaunt—Abraham Lincolnesque without the politics. This lanky Hubbell introduced a new style to baseball by wearing his trousers extremely low—practically down to his ankles. And he could throw the screwball. It was a replica of Christy Mathewson's old fadeaway. The left-hander's screwball broke away from right-handed batters and in on left-handers. Carl was not the first left-hander to employ the delivery: Hub Pruett of the St. Louis Browns had struck out Babe Ruth thirteen times with it in the season of 1922.

But the beauty of Hubbell is that he perfected the screwball without instruction while attempting to throw a sidearm sinker.

Hubbell was given a trial by the Detroit Tigers in 1926. Ty Cobb, then manager, had his coaches urge this unusual young man to abandon the screwball lest he seriously and dangerously injure his arm. But when you're young, you'll do anything. Immortality is inevitable. Deprived of "his" pitch, in the Detroit spring training, Hubbell wasn't even permitted to pitch an inning of an intra-squad contest and was shipped to Toronto, where orders had been received that he was to forget the screwball. He won 7 and lost 7 with Toronto.

The following spring, at San Antonio, Texas, where the Tigers trained, George Moriarty, former third baseman and umpire, was managing Detroit. Moriarty also took a negative view of Hubbell's screwball, and Carl was shipped down to Decatur, Illinois, of the Three I League.

Detroit, giving up on him, sold Hubbell to Beaumont, Texas. Upon joining the Texas League club, he enjoyed so much success that the Giants bought him for $25,000.

My father told me that Hubbell could throw the screwball with three different speeds and had the temerity to use it as a change of pace.

The master of the screwball was born June 22, 1903, in Carthage, Missouri. Now the screwball is a particularly special talent that I believe requires a special physical force because it is almost a defamation of nature. Hubbell's lanky body also gave him the long pliable wrist that enabled him to throw a ball by turning the left wrist to the right. In time it also permanently turned Hubbell's left hand facing the opposite direction—shades of demons.

With great clarity I remember my father coming home from the Polo Grounds late one night raving about Hubbell. It was dark, and even in my childish mind I wondered how they were able to play (arc lights were not installed until 1940 at the Polo Grounds). This was July 2, 1933, and that date produced one of the most famous doubleheaders in baseball history—Giants and St. Louis Cardinals.

In the first game, which went eighteen innings, Hubbell went the distance for the win, allowing only 6 hits, striking out twelve, and not one batter walked. The excitement my father generated made me push for more information. The Giants won 1–0. A single hit by Hughie Critz won the game. The second game was a duel between Giant right-hander Roy Parmelee and Dizzy Dean, and the only run was a fourth-inning homer by Giant third baseman Johnny Vergez.

My dad told me that Hubbell's first feat to attract attention was his no-hit game against the Pirates in 1929. It was only the start of a circus parade of achievements that included ten shutouts and a streak of forty-six consecutive scoreless innings in 1933. Then the string of 24 consecutive victories, 16 in a row by the end of 1936. On top of that 8 straight the next year. Hubbell had an earned average of 1.66 in 1933, lowest since Grover Alexander's 1.55 in 1916; and the most heralded record of all, his consecutive strike-outs of Babe Ruth, Lou Gehrig, Jimmy Foxx, Al Simmons, and Joe Cronin in the All-Star game of 1934 at the Polo Grounds.

If you're in the market for an idol, why not pick a great one; and so I became Carl Hubbell for a while. I even attempted to fool around with the screwball, but I stopped because the attempt hurt my elbow and shoulder too much. Since I had already discovered that I was an endangered species, I decided to not try to conquer the machinations of the screwball.

Hubbell supplied the anchor for the New York Giants and was

called the Meal Ticket from 1933 through 1937. This daring young man during the period of the Great Depression was going against the grain of physics and succeeding. Who would not take hope in that. With Bill Terry at the helm, Hubbell was as dominating a pitching force as the senior circuit had ever seen.

At the age of forty, Hubbell retired after the 1943 season and was immediately named director of the Giants' farm system.

Without question Carl Hubbell along with Dodgers' Sandy Koufax and Tigers' Hal Newhouser were the greatest left-handed pitchers I ever saw.

The last time I saw Hubbell was in July 1983 at the Hyatt Hotel in Chicago. I was doing a pre–All-Star WABC Sportstalk show from the lobby. With remorse, I cannot forget viewing his inability to negotiate the steps on the escalator. The tears filled my eyes. Where the hell did the time go. My boyhood hero, the magnificent one in the Polo Grounds, wound up as we all will if we're lucky enough to get to be struggling senior citizens.

Sometimes you have so many idols you don't know where to worship. I cannot leave out the Splendid Splinter, the Thumper, outfielder Ted Williams, a once-in-a-generation hitter—the best in our time. What I love about the man was that he recognized his talent and knew his art and practiced it. He had a keen appreciation of the strike zone, a great eye, quick hands—and what power. If he had not gone into the military service twice (World War II and the Korean conflict), God knows how many records he would have set.

He spent a prodigious amount of time on body-building and arm-developing exercises; thereby setting a pattern for players who followed.

The first time I saw Ted Williams was April of 1939. I was sitting in the right field bleachers at Yankee Stadium, and it was the Boston Red Sox' first visit to New York for the year. I was sitting with my pretend uncle Louis Mayers.

And there I saw this long lean Williams hit a double off of Yankee right-hander Charlie "Red" Ruffing. As young as I was, I could discern greatness.

*   *   *

They called Williams haughty and arrogant, but it has always been my contention that arrogance is applicable to the very talented who are fully aware of what they are able to produce, and I salute that. It is only ignorant or stupid arrogance that bothers me.

But there is another side to the coin. I read that Williams was a very kind and considerate person. When Ted Williams was a kid, his mother, who played the cornet in the Salvation Army Band, gave him 30 cents every morning to buy his lunch at school. However, his teachers noticed that the child seldom ate lunch and with his lean lanky frame looked undernourished. After many inquiries the teachers found that he was giving his lunch money to boys less fortunate than he. I think admirable deeds as a child show you the measure of the man.

When Williams became eligible for a loser's share of the receipts of the 1946 World Series, a matter of $2,150.89, he thought that the Red Sox clubhouse attendant, Johnny Orlando, was deserving of a tip and gave him a check for $2,500. Williams was a madman, but he had a fine madness. The kind of madness we admire in an Albert Einstein, the Wright brothers, Margaret Sanger, Marcus Garvey, and Hannibal, who somehow got elephants over the Alps.

You could never predict what the man would do, and that was part of the beauty of the whole scheme. Williams was the man sportswriters called surly, petulant, sulking, pouting, and all those adjectives of that nature. And it was true that at various times he was all of those things.

The hell with that, he was also one of the most gifted batters in the history of baseball. I remember when I was just a little kid reading a Russian fairy tale. If I remember correctly, it was about a group of people stranded on a desolate island. There was one man who could bring these people back to their civilization. The only thing was that this man had terrible sores all over his body and was abhorrent to the survivors. They had to accept him because he knew the way out. I know I am stretching an analogy, but Williams, despite his faults, when he reported to the Red Sox in the spring of 1938 was standing 6'3" in height and weighing in at 175—formidable.

When he arrived at Sarasota for spring training, he attracted immediate attention because of his cockiness, his promise of greatness, and because he refused to wear a necktie and even missed a bus to an exhibition game; but he was just a headstrong twenty-year-old. He was not ready for major league competition, and the Red Sox optioned him to Minneapolis on March 21. My God, that year playing under Donie Bush, he tore the American Association to bits. Williams hit .366 and socked 43 home runs.

He joined the big club in 1939. He gained his greatest glory in 1941: He batted .406 and blasted one of his most memorable homers. How well do I remember July 1941. My mother was ironing in the kitchen, and I'm in my room listening to the All-Star game from Briggs Stadium in Detroit. Oh boy, was I happy. I'm a National League fan, and they're ahead. Arky Vaughan has just hit his second home run for the National League. All of a sudden in the bottom of the ninth, up steps Ted Williams, who smacks one over the top of the roof in right field off Cub right-hander Claude Passeau. I remember sitting there in my room crying. Concerned, my mother came to me, and when I explained the situation, she laughed. Her response was, "What the hell are you getting so upset over the white man's game for anyway?" I love and adore my mother, but she did not understand the intensity of my feelings for the game.

On the final morning of the 1941 season, Williams had a batting average of .349 and was faced with a doubleheader against the Philadelphia Athletics at Shibe Park. In the first game he banged out 4 hits and 2 in the second, 6 in eight tries and had the distinction of becoming the first player in the American League since 1923 to hit .400 (He hit .406). As of yet there has been no equal.

What a career Williams went on to have. Two time triple crown winner, 1942 and 1947, and the only American Leaguer to do that.

Hopefully, all of us have had our great moments. Ted Williams had more than his share. In 1946 he was the league's Most Valuable Player. He hit .342 with 38 homers and 123 RBIs, and during his reign the Red Sox won their only pennant.

The man was a total phenomenon. In 1949 he hit a career high of 43 homers and had 159 RBIs and an average of .343. Only the Lord knows what he would have done the next year, but he broke his elbow in the 1950 All-Star game making a catch against the left field wall. Still, in 89 games he had 28 homers and 97 RBIs.

He went to war in 1952, but he came back. Williams hit .407 in 37 games in the 1953 season. It's incredible, but at the age of 39 in 1957 he hit .388.

When Ted Williams was inducted into the Hall of Fame in 1966, he declared, ''I hope Satchel Paige and Josh Gibson [both legendary Black players who could only work the Negro National Leagues in their time slot] will be voted into the Hall of Fame as symbols of the great Black players who are not here only because they weren't given the chance.''

God, I love a human being like Williams.

I had the ultimate pleasure of meeting Ted Williams in 1969 when he was the manager of the Washington Senators. The long, lean idol that I had so admired had a huge paunch. Then I thought, what the hell, I know damn well I don't look like I did twenty years ago, but that does not keep me from being me. There is something about growing older that says I got over that hump, now let's try for the mountain.

Ted Williams forever.

AND THE SONG GOES ON

Oh, here was another marvel, Stan Musial, outfielder for the St. Louis Cardinals—an extraordinary athlete. The first time I saw him was at the Polo Grounds in September 1941, the final month of the season. He was fresh up from the Rochester Red Wings of the International League along with third baseman Whitey Kurowski and outfielder Erv Dusak. How distinctly I recall my teacher Alexander Triffon, J.H.S. 164, who recognized my enthusiasm for the game and found we shared a mutual interest. He let me out of class early so I could see the Cardinal game and relate my impression to him the next day. Do teachers come that way anymore, or was it an exception?

As a thirteen-year-old I cornered and introduced myself to Musial. I found him to be a decent, intelligent person with a kind of laid-back drive. That September of 1941 in 12 National League games, he batted .426.

I was a groupie before it was fashionable. I followed Musial from the game that fall day down the subway steps, through the turnstile, and into the subway car. I rode all the way with him to the Astor Hotel on Forty-third Street and Broadway. He seemed pleased, and was responsive toward this Black kid who knew so much about him. I will always love Musial for that brief serendipity.

Although worlds apart, Musial reminded me of my cousin Vernon Cooper. Vernon was from Panama. Musial was the fifth of six children from a coal-mining town, Donora, Pennsylvania. I don't know where that resemblance started or stopped, but it was there.

I loved the peculiar batting stance of Musial. It was like a disco dancer getting in rhythm before the onslaught of the dance floor.

Stan Musial was the greatest of all the stars developed by Branch Rickey at St. Louis. After Cardinal scout Andy French saw him in a high school game in Donora, Pennsylvania, he signed him to a contract with Williamson, West Virginia, of the Mountain States League. It was there that Musial began his career as a left-handed pitcher.

How far Musial could have gone as a pitcher will never be known. Moved from Williamson to Daytona Beach of the Florida State League in 1940, he won 18 and lost 5. But because of his strong hitting, he was employed in the outfield on days he did not pitch. In a game against Orlando in August 1940, he damaged his left shoulder in making a diving catch, and that was the end of him as a pitcher.

In the spring of 1941 the St. Louis Cardinals held a mass training camp for minor league players at Columbus, Georgia. It was there that Musial showed ability with the bat, but his lame left arm made him a question mark. Burt Shotton decided his future lay in the outfield, and on that basis he was assigned to Springfield of the Western Association.

Musial batted .379 in a half season at Springfield, then was moved up to Rochester of the International League. There he hit .326 in 54 games and was advanced to the Cardinals in September to aid in the pennant drive.

Before Musial's twenty-two-year career came to an end in 1963, he established a bushel basket of senior circuit records. Musial led the National League in batting seven times, in hits six times, in doubles seven times and triples five times. Voted the league's Most Valuable Player in 1943, '46, and '48, he was one of the most sensitive, decent, and congenial of the superstars. These qualities I first came upon at the Polo Grounds and on that Eighth Avenue subway car in September 1941.

Stan the Man was some kind of a ballplayer.

*   *   *

AND THE SONG GOES ON

As the main cog in the St. Louis Cardinal infield and the "tenth man" on the team, Marty Marion was the dominant factor in their winning back-to-back-to-back pennants in 1942, '43, and '44. His fielding was without peer among a long line of star shortstops, and without his uncanny ability of turning seemingly safe hits into outs on both sides of the field, the Cardinal pitchers would have found their road to victory much more difficult.

Although nervous as a cat in his actions, Marion always was as steady as a clock in the field. Called a human octopus, the 6'5" 170-pound Cardinal shortstop from Richburg, South Carolina, was a steadying influence on the entire team, and it is doubtful, despite the ease with which they won the pennant, that the Redbirds would have had anything but a desperate battle to finish in front without him.

The Richburg, South Carolina, stringbean was one of the greatest defensive shortstops of all time. He was the best I ever saw. Marion was a long, lanky fellow with great range, a good pair of hands, and a good accurate arm. Even from deep short, he could throw a perfect strike to first base. He could come in on a ball, go behind second, do everything with the glove. And from an "out" man at the plate, he improved so much, learning to hit to the opposite field, that he became a tough man in the clutch, and one year he even led the league in doubles.

I will never forget a 1942 doubleheader at the Polo Grounds . . . . The Cardinals swept two from the Giants that day. The brilliant performance of Marion that Sunday afternoon left no doubt in my mind about his greatness. He went left, he went right like some elongated vacuum cleaner. He didn't need a third baseman or a second baseman. All he needed was a first baseman to throw to, and that was Johnny Hopp that particular day.

Marion joined the Cardinals in 1940, fresh up from the Rochester Red Wings of the International League. He won the shortstop job and batted .278 as a rookie in 125 games. The following season he played all 155 games, batted .252, and established himself as the best at the position. He played over 100 games at shortstop every year from 1940 through 1950. In 1944 Marion won the National League's Most Valuable Player award with a .267 average as the Cardinals won their third pennant in a row. The award was a testimony to his awesome defensive play.

Marion managed the Cardinals in 1951 and did not play. He returned to the field in 1952 and 1953 as a player and manager with the St. Louis Browns.

In 1940 Marion "influenced" me with something that would last the rest of my life. I'd written a letter to him requesting an autographed picture. He answered with the photo and a brief note . . . in which he circled his *i*'s rather than dotting them. I've done the same ever since.

In the last ten years Marty and I have become close personal friends. He's been a guest on my sports show on WABC many, many times. Marty presently is in charge of the restaurant in Busch Stadium in St. Louis.

Marty Marion along with Mark Belanger and Roy McMillan are the greatest defensive shortstops I ever saw.

I would be remiss if I didn't mention the greatest defensive center fielder that I ever saw. He was Terry Moore of the St. Louis Cardinals. He was the nonpareil of outfielders.

If Moore had cavorted on the diamonds of New York City, Polo Grounds, Yankee Stadium, or Ebbets Field, he would have been hailed as the second coming of Jesus Christ.

Moore was a great team leader as well as a helluva competitor.

He was a timely hitter who'll best be remembered for his defensive brilliance; his ham-sized hands; accurate arm (the late baseball writer J. Roy Stockton once said that "Terry Moore could throw a ball into a bucket at a hundred yards"); and ability to scoop up ground balls like an infielder.

I'll never forget a gorgeous Saturday afternoon in October 1942. It was game number three of the Yankee/Cardinal World Series, at the big ball orchid in the South Bronx. My father and I were sitting in the right field bleachers in the Yankee Stadium. In the Yankee seventh, Joe DiMaggio hit a rising line shot to left center. Cardinals left fielder Stan Musial fell down in pursuit of the ball, and subsequently Moore, backing Musial up, made an incredible sideways catch practically at right angles to the ground. It was without a doubt the second greatest grab that I ever saw in World Series competition. I'd have to call Giant Willie Mays's capture of Indian Vic Wertz's wallop in game one of the 1954 fall classic number one.

The 5'11" 195-pound Terry Bluford Moore was born in Vernon, Alabama, in 1912, and from 1935 to 1948 Moore, a clone of onetime movie actor Dick Foran, was the bulwark of the St. Louis Cardinal outer garden, anchoring Stan Musial to his right and Enos Slaughter to his left for eight of those years.

One of my disappointing memories of Moore was an incident twenty-nine years ago when the Cardinals were in town to play the Giants. I called their hotel to ask Charlie Peete to be on my show at WWRL. Peete was one of the three Black players on the Cardinal team. The others were outfielder Chuck Harmon and first baseman Tom Alston. It was 1956, and perhaps a large percentage of America hadn't gotten used to the fact that Blacks and whites all shared a commonality.

Well, anyway, the telephone operator inadvertently connected me with Terry Moore's room. When I said Charlie Peete, Moore responded, "Oh, you want the colored guy." There is something disparaging in that remark. He just should have said, "You have the wrong room." That I could take. At least I will give him credit for being embarrassed when I said, "Look, I'm colored too." Ah, what the hell, I'm used to it by this time.

The accomplishment of the New York Giants in 1951 was ever so much greater than that of the "miracle" Boston Braves in 1914. George Stallings's club had extricated itself from the cellar, 15 games out of first place, on July 6 to win the pennant, true enough, but that's not the real story. The flag chase of 1914 was so tight that the Braves, though second on August 10, were only 6½ games out of first place. The Giants of 1951 on August 11 found themselves 13½ games behind the Dodgers. Even after winning 16 in a row, they were still 6 games out.

Early in the campaign it appears that manager Leo Durocher, for all his moves in rebuilding, was going to be greatly disappointed. In the first few weeks of the season, the Giants dropped eleven straight ball games. But in the latter part of May, the team called up Willie Mays, a sensational young outfielder from Minneapolis. Mays started slowly at bat, although he was brilliant defensively with his sparkling catches and throws. Durocher stayed with him, built his confidence, and the Giants had a Black star who would rival the Brooklyn Dodgers' Jackie Robinson and Roy Campanella.

In his first twenty-two trips to the plate in 1951, Willie went hitless. He finally went to Durocher in desperation and asked to be taken out of the lineup. Durocher responded, "You're my center fielder if you don't get a hit the rest of the season." By season's end, Willie had hit 20 home runs and knocked in 68. The Giants, much like Willie, made one of the most remarkable comebacks in baseball history that season. The Giants caught and tied the Dodgers on the last day of the season and beat the Dodgers in a 3-game playoff climaxed by Bobby Thomson's home run in the bottom of the ninth inning. The pennant came to New York, and Willie won the National League's award for Rookie of the Year.

The first time I saw Willie Mays was early in May 1951. He was catching fungoes in the outfield at the Polo Grounds. You could feel the electricity emanating from the man. You could note and respond to a sense of greatness that particular day. I was right, as well as many millions easily discerned.

But despite the acknowledgment of Mays's obvious talent, I cling to the image of Joe "D." I think this is part and parcel of what you grow up with. Perfection to me was DiMaggio, Nat King Cole, Duke Ellington. I could not figure out how to equate Mays, this young kid, in the scheme of my design of existence: His hat flew off when he was making a catch: not cool; Joe D's hat never fell off. That's a perfectly silly reason not to admire the rareness of special ability. Yes, he was as good as and possibly better than one of my idols.

Perhaps I had so many idols I almost felt like a pagan.

On May 6, 1931, Willie Howard Mays was born in Westfield, Alabama. His father was a professional player in the Negro leagues. I am confident that he was an inspiration for his young son.

In 1952 he was drafted into the army. When he returned to baseball in 1954—look out, he tore it apart. In 151 games he batted

.345 with 195 hits, 41 home runs and 110 RBIs, and the Giants again won the pennant.

In the World Series against the American League champion Cleveland Indians, he again did the impossible; he made an unbelievable catch of a drive off the bat of Vic Wertz. Mays raced to deep center field, approximately 460 feet from home plate, stuck up his glove, and made the catch people are still talking about today.

How well do I remember 1954! I was broadcasting sports for station WWRL at Small's Paradise, a favorite watering hole and entertainment center in Harlem. Small's at that time was a remnant of what Harlem used to be. It was a carryover from the days of glory of Harlem and Striver's Row. Ah, Striver's Row, therein were contained 106 luxurious brownstones built by Frank Lloyd Wright on 138th and 139th streets.

Anyway, I interviewed Willie about that fabulous catch at Small's.

The Giants won that 1954 World Series in 4 games.

After the game I did a tape with Mays in the Giant clubhouse, and he had this to say about the catch. . . .

"I turned my back and ran, looked over my shoulder once to gauge the flight of the ball, then kept running. I grabbed the ball the way a football wide receiver catches a long pass. Then I spun and threw. Davey Williams came out to take the relay, and then Larry Doby managed to tag and go to third, while Al Rosen didn't go anywhere. If anything, I think my throw was the remarkable thing, because the ball got back to the infield in a helluva hurry, and I was a good four hundred fifty feet out when I caught it."

Mays had an electrifying quality that inspired his club, an intangible effect that cannot be seen in batting averages or fielding records.

The Giants left New York in 1958 as Horace Stoneham, owner-president, moved West to San Francisco. Willie followed. Along the trail between 1951 and 1973, Willie established himself as a future occupant of the Hall of Fame. He led the league in home runs four times, hitting his season high of 52 in 1965. He was third in career home runs with 660, third only to Hank Aaron and Babe Ruth. Then he proceeded to bat over .300 ten different seasons. Willie was named the National League's most valuable player in 1954. He was named to the National League's All-Star season from 1954 to 1973. He hit 4 home runs in one game in 1961 (that's really socking it to you), tying the major league record. It was fitting that Willie should end his career in New York. He joined the New York Mets in May 1972 in a trade that sent Charlie Williams to the Giants along with $50,000. Moreover, the Mets contract with him gave Mays lifetime security. He made an auspicious debut with the Mets against his former teammates on May 14. With the score tied at 4–4, Mays sent a long drive over the wall in left center field to gain the game for the Mets.

At a packed house at Shea Stadium, Willie in September of 1973 announced his retirement with tears in his eyes.

Good fellow well met.

And then there was another man who had a raw Tarzanlike strength. There was no one like Mickey Mantle. When he hit the rock, it was smitten. Mantle was sullen, mean, and difficult. But what do we measure, the man or the ability of the man?

He was great, and I wonder about the marvel of it. I don't know how many times I've seen the late Yankee trainer Gus Mauch tape up Mantle's legs like a mummy before each game. Mantle was a victim of chronic osteomyelitis, a bone inflammation of his left foot. And then when he was in his first season with the Yankees (1951), he sustained an injury to the right knee. There has to be something about a man who had to endure that kind of pain and still come up a winner. I admired his endurance.

He was born in Spavinaw, Oklahoma, on October 20, 1931. His father's hero was Detroit catcher Mickey Cochrane, and starstruck, he named his son Mickey. Almost from day one he was dealing with a ball.

Mantle was always an outstanding athlete from the age of seven, and by the time he reached high school he was a phenomenon, a hero. They say if you build a better mousetrap, the world will beat a path to your door. And so scout Tom Greenwade of the Yankees went to see. He watched a sandlot game that Mantle participated in, and a contract was signed that day.

Mantle was an inaccurate-throwing shortstop in Independence and Joplin, Missouri, before he reported to the Yankees in the spring of 1951. But at the Yankee camp in Phoenix, Arizona, manager Casey Stengel took one look at him and named Mantle to the outfield. Stengel had a good eye.

Though the potential was obvious, the rough edges had to be smoothed. Former Yankee right fielder turned coach Tommy Henrich, along with Casey Stengel, as well as Joe DiMaggio in his last season, contributed highly to his development, showing him how to catch fly balls and bolstering his confidence in his infinite ability.

Oh, boy, in his first year he hit some significant home runs, but by the same token he also struck out a lot. The raw talent was there and needed honing. After the All-Star break he was sent to Kansas City to gain more knowledge about the strike zone. The pennant fight was on, and the Yankees could not afford the privilege of giving Mantle experience at their expense.

So we have this twenty-year-old young man, the high school hero and accepted by a major league club as a kid, demoted to their farm team, the Kansas City Blues. His depression was so great that scout Tom Greenwade was commissioned to go to Kansas City to cheer up Mantle.

That proved to be a charm. Mantle's batting average lifted to .361, and he had a fantastic total of 50 RBIs in 40 games before the Yankees recalled him.

Although Mantle played in the World Series against the Giants that year, he went hitless in the first game but beat out an infield hit in the second. Then, in the fifth inning of that contest, Willie Mays hit a routine fly ball to right center. Mickey was playing alongside of DiMaggio in center, and both started for the ball; suddenly Mantle fell to the ground as though in a faint; he lay there motionless as DiMaggio caught the ball and ran to his side.

Joe D rushed to the prostrate Mickey and motioned for the stretcher, which carted Mickey from the field. I was in the ball yard that day, and it gave me a sinking feeling.

Portents of things to come. Mantle's right knee had given out from under him, and he remained motionless: He was afraid he had broken his leg. (Actually, he had torn cartilage in the knee.) The knee was operated on, and Mickey was a regular with the Yankees the next season.

Mantle's medical report: 1951, right knee cartilage operation; 1954, knee cyst removed; 1955, pulled groin muscle; 1956, left knee sprain; 1957, right shoulder injury; 1959, broken finger; 1961, hip abscess; 1962, left knee injury; 1963, broken metatarsal bone in left foot; 1965, right shoulder, right elbow, and left knee surgery.

Mantle could hit a baseball farther than anybody I ever saw play the game. From the right side of the plate, his swing was a level one that produced "frozen ropes" that outfielders didn't have a chance to get to. From the port side, Mickey crushed low pitches, golfing them unbelievable distances.

His most famous right-handed home run happened in Washington's Griffith Stadium in 1953. Mantle smashed a pitch by Senator left-hander Chuck Stobbs that cleared the fence in front of the center field stands, kept climbing, cleared the front wall of the stands, climbed a little higher, and bounced off the edge of a signboard atop the stands. Yankee press agent Arthur "Red" Patterson measured the shot. He came up with the figure of 565 feet.

In 1956 he hit a ball almost completely out of the Yankee Stadium off Washington Senator right-hander Pedro Ramos, the ball bouncing off the facade of the roof in right field less than a yard from the top. It struck the roof 355 feet from home plate and about 105 feet above the level of the playing field.

WPIX veteran TV baseball cameraman Duilio Costabile told me that he found it difficult to follow a Mantle home run blow with his camera. He said the ball literally rocketed out of the park, "voom, voom, voom."

At the 1964 World Series between the St. Louis Cardinals and the New York Yankees at the Yankee Stadium, I had the opportunity to privately interview Mantle. I asked Mantle what he thought about the brilliant ball playing of Lou Brock. Brock, who is Black, was the catalytic agent that propelled the Cards to the pennant after he was purchased from the Chicago Cubs in June of the 1964 season.

I was startled when Mantle's responses seemed to generate an air of disdain. But I was much younger then and perhaps I didn't realize the effectiveness of the Black power movement. The year 1964 was an era of Black protestation and rightful demonstration. Names like Stokely Carmichael, Rap Brown, Malcolm X, and of course Dr. Martin Luther King exploded and erupted into what I now consider a "kind" revolution. But on the other hand, an awareness was developed by the white populace, and perhaps an inch of oppression was overcome.

But perhaps in response, Mantle resisted my queries with what I considered a racist reaction. He responded to my question about Lou Brock by ignoring the question asked and proceeded to tell me about the white ballplayers on the Cardinals, mainly Ken Boyer, Tim McCarver, Dick Groat, certainly good men all. I felt his tirade was uncalled for, but I also knew why.

Perhaps a young man from Spavinaw, Oklahoma, could not realize or recognize the rage that his Black brethren had endured and to which they had finally said "enough." Sometimes that's tough to swallow much less understand.

Despite his foibles, which we all have, Mantle went on to baseball glory. He hit 536 homers, four league home run titles, and three Most Valuable Player Awards.

In World Series competition, he hit a record 18 home runs and a record-setting 40 runs batted in.

Mickey was inducted into the Hall of Fame in 1974.

Jesus Christ! I'm sitting in front of my TV set, and Hank Aaron has just broken Babe Ruth's home run record. As the tears of joy stream from my eyes, I know this has to be my ultimate sports thrill . . . and that's saying a lot. I was sitting in Section 22 at the Polo Grounds when Bobby Thomson hit it out against the Dodgers; I was in the Yankee Stadium for Don Larsen's perfect game in the World Series; thrilled to many great Sugar Ray Robinson performances; went ecstatic over Jimmy Brown's scoring three touchdowns against the Giants at the Yankee Stadium in 1963. But this home run by Aaron has to be the tops!

It all started April 23, 1954. Hank Aaron hit his first major league homer off Vic Raschi of the St. Louis Cardinals. On Monday evening April 3, 1974, Henry Aaron ended the great pursuit and passed George Herman Babe Ruth as the leading home run hitter in baseball history when he hit number 715 before a national television audience and 53,775 on hand in Atlanta Stadium.

AARON HITS 714, TIES THE BABE *(New York Daily News* headline, April 5, 1974)

AARON BLASTS 715th HOMER IN ATLANTA AND BREAKS RUTH'S RECORD (The *New York Times* headline, April 9, 1974)

The forty-year-old Atlanta Braves' outfielder broke the record on his second swing of a noisy evening. It was a soaring line drive in the fourth inning off lefty Al Downing of the Los Angeles Dodgers. It cleared the fence in left center field, some 385 feet from home plate. ("I have never gone out on a ball field and given less than my level best. When I hit it tonight, all I thought about was that I wanted to touch all the bases.")

As the man from Mobile jogged around the bases after hitting his 715 major league home run, in a career that began twenty-five years ago with the Indianapolis Clowns, in the old Negro leagues, a skyrocket arched over the jammed stadium. It was seven minutes after nine o'clock, some thirty-nine years after Ruth had hit his 714 and four days after Aaron had hit his 714 on his first swing of the bat in the season's opener.

Henry was born on February 5, 1934, in Mobile, Alabama, the third of eight children born to Herbert and Estelle Aaron. In his grammar school days Aaron was a catcher for one of the clubs in the Louisiana Recreation League. When he entered Central High School, he had to play softball, since the school could not afford equipment for a hardball team. He played shortstop, third base, and catcher for the softball team and was an outstanding footballer as a halfback and end. After two years at Central, he transferred to Allen Institute, a private school in Mobile. It wasn't until his junior year in high school that Aaron got his first chance to play ball on a semipro level. Henry played for the Mobile Black Bears, and on the final Sunday of the season the Bears met the Indianapolis Clowns. The Clowns were so impressed with Aaron's performance that they offered him $200 a month to play for them the following year.

Aaron led the Negro American League his first season with the Clowns by hitting .467. Strangely enough, Aaron was batting crosshanded at this time, a habit he corrected long before he came up to the majors. After watching Aaron play a Negro league game in 1952, Milwaukee Braves scout Dewey Griggs recommended Aaron to the Braves general manager, John Quinn. The Braves then purchased Aaron for $2,500 down and $7,500 later.

In 1952 he played with the Braves' farm club at Eau Claire in the Northern League. In 87 games he hit .336, which was good enough to earn him Rookie of the Year and a place on the All-Star team.

In 1953 Aaron moved up to Jacksonville in the Class A Sally League. He literally tore apart the South Atlantic League pitching. He led the league in batting (.362), hits (208), runs (115), runs batted in (125).

Aaron was a second baseman his one year at Jacksonville, but Milwaukee had a plethora of infield prospects in the organization and put him in the outfield during the off season while he was playing winter ball in the Puerto Rican League.

During the winter the Braves purchased outfielder Bobby Thomson from the Giants, and it then looked like another year in the minor leagues for Aaron. But during spring training Thomson suffered a triple fracture of his right ankle sliding into second base, and Aaron replaced him in the outfield. Henry hit .280 and drove in 69 runs before he too suffered a broken ankle, in September. He recuperated quickly, and the following season he hit .314, 27 homers, and batted in 106 runs.

Aaron won the batting championship in 1956, hitting .328. The Braves, however, lost the flag on the last day of the season. In 1957 Hank led the league in home runs with 44, and the Braves won the National League championship. Hank was voted the National League's Most Valuable Player. It was a great year for

Aaron. He hit .322 and drove in 132 runs. One of the highlights of his career happened on the night of September 23. The Braves were playing the St. Louis Cardinals. With the score tied in the eleventh inning, Henry came up with one on. He then hit Billy Muffett's fastball over the center field fence. His home run won the game and the pennant. At the age of twenty-three, Hank Aaron was already a superstar.

In 1966 the Braves migrated to Atlanta. Hank hit 44 home runs his first year there. Subsequently, that '66 season paid off in his receiving his first $100,000 contract. That year on April 20 in Philadelphia, he hit home run 400. In 1968 his round-trip total reached 500. Shortly thereafter he passed Mickey Mantle and started gaining on Willie Mays. Then people began to think he had a chance to catch Babe Ruth.

In 1969 in the playoffs against the Mets, Henry hit 3 home runs in a losing cause. In 1970 Henry collected his 3,000 base hit. He hit 47 home runs in 1971, batted .327, and drove in 118 runs. Before the 1972 campaign Hank signed a new contract with Atlanta. It was for $200,000, making him the highest-paid player in baseball history (at the time) and deservedly so.

Aaron was one of major league baseball's best all-around performers, the game's greatest home run swinger and runs-batted-inner, an excellent glove man, fine base runner, and the perfect team man.

In 1974 after hitting homers 714 and 715, Aaron finished out that season with 20 homers for the Braves and then was traded back to Milwaukee, now an American League club, as the DH (designated hitter). In two seasons in the junior circuit, Aaron hit 22 home runs. He finished his career with 755.

Aaron was elected to the Hall of Fame in 1982.

In the spring of 1984 I saw Bob Gibson in the Atlanta Braves' dugout when the New York Mets were playing in that southern town. The sight of Bob dredged up memories of our last encounter of importance. The occasion was the funeral of Ellie Howard, the first Black signed by the New York Yankees in 1955.

After the services at a Madison Avenue establishment, Gibson, Bill White, and I stopped for a bit of libation at a nearby pub.

Gibby was in a deep funk. He was bitter, tough, surly in his attitude about people in general and baseball in particular. His vitriolic rage exploded at what he considered the hypocrisy of the baseball people who were sanctimoniously heaping praise on the now deceased man. Gibson pointed out that there were those who too late were saying that Ellie should have been a major league manager. The entire baseball establishment received the brunt of his venom.

As mean and as truculent as Gibson was in that bar, he was the same way on the baseball tundra. He was the original "bad dude." He had taken this gift life presented to him and done more with it than most men. Without question, Gibson had to be one of the finest right-handed pitchers we ever saw. His skill, coordination, and intelligence encompassed all sports—a true natural.

Bob Gibson was another one of those extraordinary men who refused to be trapped in what destiny signaled. I've heard the story so many times that it has assumed the aura of a myth—the Black woman with six or seven children, widowed or deserted. This woman has "low-value" skills that seldom earn enough to feed her family. Yet from somewhere she scratches and kicks the hell out of destiny and raises giants.

Bob Gibson was born on November 19, 1935, in Omaha, Nebraska. At 6'11" and 190 pounds, he was one of Nebraska's finest all-around athletes. Gibson played baseball, basketball, football and ran track, all with equal facility. He won a scholarship to Creighton University, played with the Harlem Globetrotters for one year, then signed with the St. Louis Cardinals in 1957.

He spent three years in the Cardinal chain and another three with the big club before becoming an established starting pitcher.

Gibson's forte was a blazing fastball that when it was all over led him to a National League career record of 3,117 strikeouts. The inability to control his fastball handicapped him his first two major league campaigns, but by 1961 he had enough control of the pitch to win 13 games, starting a skein of fourteen straight years in which he won more than 10 games each year.

How can anyone forget the performance of Gibson in 1968? He won 22 games, 13 of them shutouts, led the league with 268 strikeouts, and had an earned run average of 1.12. And he capped his fantastic year by striking out a record 17 batters in the opening contest of the World Series.

The hard-throwing Gibson, who won 251 games in his major league career, was elected to the Hall of Fame in 1981.

Life to me has been a revelation realized through the aspect of sports. It started with my father's enthusiasm for sports and his consequent invasion of my mind for the love for a relatively passive form of conquest. My now deceased junkie of baseball, Georgie Vaz, and I shared a common bondage. Whenever I think of Georgie I almost weep when I recall the untroubled joyous boyhood, reflections of which sustain me now in more complex times. Now I look forward to the new recollections I may live long enough to enjoy: the prowess of outfielder Darryl Strawberry of the New York Mets; pitcher Dwight Gooden of the New York Mets; outfielder–first baseman Don Mattingly of the New York Yankees; pitcher Jose Rijo of the New York Yankees.

I praise the memories that that old viscount stickball club dredge up: my cousin Irving Rust, now a gynecologist, Roy Cobb an insurance executive, Leon Bogues a state senator, Ernest Cobb a sales executive, Junior Manning a maître' d of a major New York hotel, Sonny Curtis a retired police officer.

I think we turned out to be a pretty good group—perhaps a motley crew, but we had the common denominator of baseball, stickball that imbued certainly a sense of competitiveness, camaraderie, and a desire to increase skills that may have spilled over to make our lives different.

Down the Art Rust, Jr., turnpike I have found the quintessence of sports is merely one of the many abstractions of survival.

INDEX

175

INDEX

INDEX

INDEX

INDEX

INDEX